The Secret Landscapes

Clara Brack

Clara Brack was born in Melbourne in 1949, the first of four daughters of artists Helen Maudsley and John Brack. After an Arts degree at Melbourne University, she taught in Technical Schools and then TAFE. She also wrote and took photographs, making books for family and friends. In 2014, she self-published *The Eye Sees Not Itself*. *The Secret Landscapes* is the result of over twenty years of writing releasing herself from inhibitions about putting her story into a public place.

Clara Brack

The Secret Landscapes

On Not Pleasing your Mother

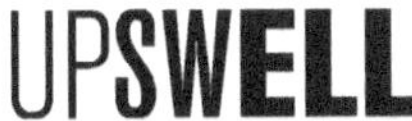

First published in Australia in 2026
by Upswell Publishing
Perth, Western Australia
upswellpublishing.com

Upswell operates in the city of Perth, on ancient country of the Whadjuk people of the Noongar nation who remain the spiritual and cultural custodians of this beautiful land. We acknowledge their continuing connection to country and express gratitude to elders past and present for their strength and creativity…Always was, always will be, Aboriginal land.

ISBN: 978-1-7642397-3-8

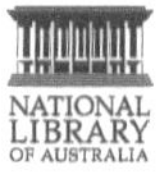

A catalogue record for this book is available from the National Library of Australia

Cover design by Chil3, Fremantle
Typeset in Foundry Origin by Lasertype
Printed by Lightning Source

Upswell Publishing is assisted by the State of Western Australia through its funding program for arts and culture.

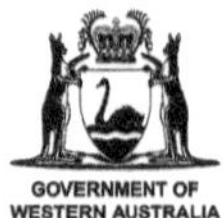

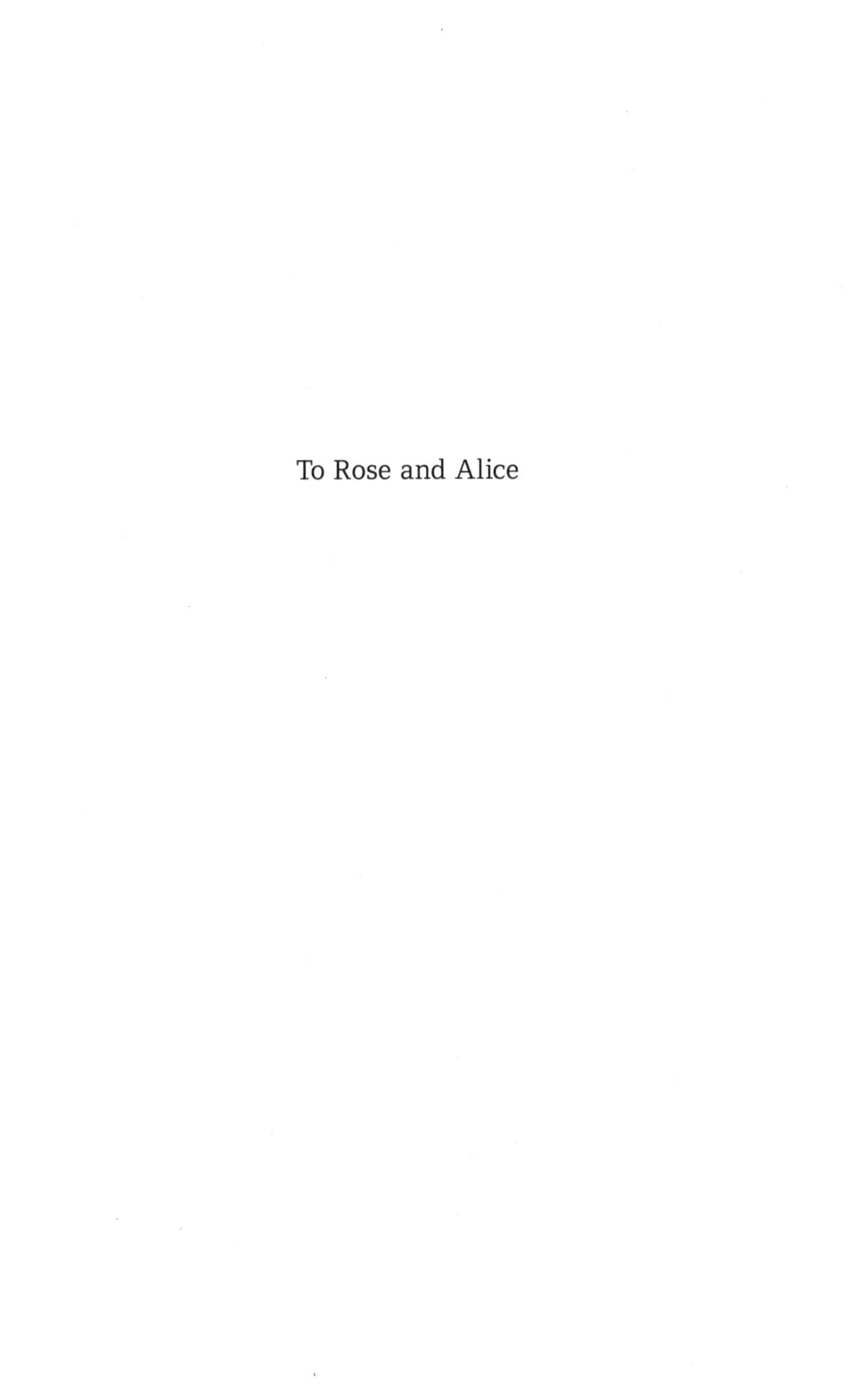

To Rose and Alice

Art is theft, art is armed robbery, art is not pleasing your mother.

Janet Malcolm

Introduction

My parents are artists John Brack and Helen Maudsley. They met at art school and exhibited their work in Melbourne from the 1950s for fifty years. My father was born in 1920, my mother in 1927. My father's work was well known. School students wrote essays on his painting *Collins St 5pm*. When asked if my father was John Brack I would sometimes say, 'My mother's an artist, too. Helen Maudsley.' 'Oh is she? I don't know her work, never heard of her.'

'Why don't you write a book about your parents?' a friend once asked me, knowing that I wrote books for family and friends. Sasha Grishin had written a book about Dad's work. A book proposed on Mum's work never eventuated. I imagined that after Mum's death a 'real' writer would do some research, interview artists and friends, look at the paintings, read what my parents had said and written about their work, and then come up with an engaging account of their lives together, of how his work was well known but hers wasn't. It would tell the story of two artists in a formative time of Australian art.

I imagined that the real writer would face the usual obstacles of writing a biography, exacerbated and enriched by it being a double biography. I imagined they would be free of the struggles I faced with my own writing. I was envious of the expertise of this writer despite the fact that this accomplished book existed only in my imagination.

When the real writer had finished this book, he or she would move onto the next while I would still be puddling along in the margins having been interviewed for that one.

There is one significant difference between me and this imaginary writer, apart from the fact of never having published a book. I have been shaped by my parents, by the relationship between them. If I were to write a book, I would make this part of the subject. I would explore the obstacles that inhibited my writing—my father's voice in me, 'you dill', and my mother's 'private is private' which, for many years, swamped my capacity to imagine or to allow myself to find my own voice.

There are also the gifts. The gift of being brought up in a home with original paintings on the walls, of seeing the inner life of my parents in their paintings, of the encouragement to make things, to invent, to break from convention. The gift of seeing the illusoriness of fame and what it takes to resist it. The gift of knowing the tenacity and the discipline required to continue working despite negative reviews and little interest in the work. The gift of knowing that art is simply hours and hours in the studio working alone.

There are the gifts and then there is the legacy we carry.

If I were to write such a book, how would I start? I would start by describing an experience that the 'real' writer would not face—the disjunction between the artist as a parent and the artist in their work.

*

I am in an art gallery looking at a painting. It's a fresco. It depicts a landscape draped with a piece of folded fabric reminiscent of the Renaissance masters. The sea shimmers with the hint of gold. The fresco radiates a mysterious tranquillity unlike any of the paintings I grew up with. I want to buy it but the man I need to see is speaking on the phone. He ignores me. Since I was brought up not to interrupt the important man, I do not interrupt him. I look around the gallery, waiting for him to finish speaking, but I am not prepared to hang around any longer, hoping to avoid the peak-hour journey home.

The next day I ring the gallery and tell the man that I want to buy the fresco. I give him my name and the numbers on the credit card.

'Are you any relation to John Brack?'

'He's my father.'

'Oh. He's my favourite Australian artist. I love *Collins Street 5pm*. I love the pictures of the postcards and the pencils.'

As he continues a glowing appraisal of my father's work, I visualise my father pacing the hallway of our family home, clenching his fists, wrestling with himself in morose melancholy.

This man loved my father's work.

Others were not so enamoured. 'I can't imagine how you live with that hanging on the wall.'

My parents' paintings formed the landscape of my childhood. Dad's paintings were hung in the room visitors would enter, Mum's were in the children's bedroom and in the hallway. Their paintings were not joyously spontaneous, paint flung onto the canvas haphazardly. They were painted with meticulous control like the disciplined routine of our household. When friends ask me, 'Do you like your parents' paintings?' I mumble something about not being able to distinguish their paintings from my experience of the artists as my mother and father.

When my mother saw the fresco I had bought, she looked at it for a moment and then said, 'It doesn't have any conflict in it.'

She said it like a chef declaring that the meal was lacking salt. She seemed puzzled, suggesting that a work of art devoid of conflict had no meaning to her. The absence of conflict may have been what drew me to the fresco. It is not 'cerebral' as Dad's paintings were known. It is not 'serious' in the way that Mum defines 'serious'. It takes us into the natural world, the mystery, the unknown.

*

The friend who suggested writing a book on my parents had proposed I write about 'what it was like watching your mother and father painting, how they got their ideas, the secrets, the funny stories, the affairs'.

'Have you ever looked at their paintings?' I thought to myself. 'Do you think a child of those artists would even consider writing this sort of book?'

I understood the curiosity to know about the lives of the people called 'artists'. The art is mysterious. A secret about the artist's life could shed light on the mystery of the work. If we feel we know the artist in the work, we feel we are entitled to know about the person who made the work. Furthermore, artists are given licence to step outside the 'bourgeois' rules other people follow. The secrets, the affairs.

My mother and my father were adamant that the artist's work speaks for itself. Dad would repeat: 'Everything to know about me is in the paintings.' Mum would repeat: 'Private is private, public is public.' For both of them, the private life of the artist was out of bounds. Besides, any artist would rather the interest was in the work, not the secret affair or what they got up to during the weekend. Nevertheless, I was mystified by the vehemence of my mother's insistence 'private is private'. As I saw it, there was nothing that warranted the urgency to keep something secret. When Dad was not at work teaching, he was busy painting. Mum went into her painting room after we left for school and reappeared when we returned. We had dinner the same time every night. We took our library books back on the due date. Neither my mother nor my father had the temperament to dance on the table and were far too responsible and dutiful to run off with other people's husbands or wives. As Dad has said in an interview, 'Some people would think of it as a boring life going into the studio day after day, six days a week, but for me it is fulfilling.'

I found myself thinking, 'All right, I will write a book about the secrets, the affairs.' I would start the book with making my mother visible but since few people knew of her work, I would surrender to starting with what the reader would know: a story about my father.

My Father

I would give my father a secret life. He would have a lover. I would call her Sonya. He would meet her on the train. He will ask her what she is reading. She will be reading *Anna Karenina* in Russian. Dad was entranced by the Ballets Russes when it came to Melbourne when he was eighteen. Sonya will have defected from the Ballets Russes. She will work as a translator commuting to the city from a cottage in the country. My father will visit her every second weekend. One day during lunch he will complain about not having a studio. Sonya will turn towards the window, wave her fork and say, 'Why don't you paint landscapes?'

If the writing were to have meaning for me it would have to have a purpose. It would have to fulfil some need in me. It would have to be inspired by my curiosity rather than answering to someone else's needs.

I am one of four daughters. Clara, Vicky, Freda and Charlotte. We sometimes speculated on what it would be like if there was a boy in our family. This was my opportunity to find out. My father will have a son with Sonya. He will stop seeing his son after the ending of the affair. He will leave the landscape paintings in Sonya's house. One of his landscape paintings will be on the cover of the book.

The son will not commit suicide as my mother predicted when we speculated on having a boy in our family. 'He could never live up to

John's expectations.' In his early twenties, the son will seek out the father he never knew. My father will write letters responding to his son's questions about his parents, the son's grandparents, about how he became an artist, about his paintings.

One morning I found myself embarking on writing the letters my father wrote to the son he never had.

As the letters progressed, I put aside the obstacles until I could no longer avoid them. For the very reason that my father did not have this secret life, I could not imagine it. It was beyond what I knew of him. It was inconceivable that he would have a lover. The fantasy of his secret life demanded that I exceed the limits of the suspension of disbelief.

I abandoned the idea for what it was—a provocative response to a suggestion to write a book about 'the secrets, the funny stories, the affairs'.

*

I read that John Brack had 'bravely stopped painting having said all that he wanted to say'. I understood that he had stopped painting because periodically the paintbrush slipped from his hand. Mum had locked his studio and hidden the keys to prevent him from continuing his attempts to 'improve' his paintings.

He had dementia from alcoholism.

A few years later he died, aged seventy-nine.

When Dad was first diagnosed with dementia, Mum became his carer. She performed this task with amazing fortitude and dedication but also with understandable resentment. To give her a break I offered to take him away for three hours on Sunday afternoons. He had trouble walking and did not like to be near other people, so I opted for a drive in the country. Dad had once painted a picture called *The Car*, a picture of a father and mother in the front seat, a boy and a girl in the back looking out the window. The trees through the car window suggest that they are driving in the country. For most of my childhood we didn't have a car. Now we were belatedly doing what other families did, this time with the daughter driving.

In the attempts at 'conversation', I asked Dad about painting. Sometimes he was lucid, revealing little snippets I doubt he would have revealed were it not for the dementia.

'Helen has taken all my money. She has put it into her bank account. She has taken it, you know, because I am successful and she is not. I feel sorry for Helen. She did not get the recognition she deserves but she paints in her own private language. She's an artist's artist. She works so hard, you know. She is very, very serious about her work. I am successful and she is not. So, that's why I haven't any money now.'

Sometimes on our walks he stopped and looked at me in terror. 'We have to go home. She will be so angry with me. I don't know what I have done wrong.'

At the time I assumed it was Mum who would be 'so angry'. Later I wondered whether it may have been his mother.

After returning him safely, I felt the disappointment of not getting what I had secretly hoped for: some meaningful connection. I had rarely spent more than two or three hours with my father alone. By the time I was permitted three hours, he had lost his mind.

'Do you have any regrets?' I asked him on one of the drives, hoping he would say, 'I wish I spent more time with you children.'

'I wish I had painted with more confidence like Picasso.'

My anger was palpable. I wish I had lived with more confidence in myself, like those whose fathers said, 'well done'. I remember thinking, 'I could stop the car, open the door, push him out and keep driving.' He would offer no resistance.

Once, when we had ended up at Shoreham Maze, we walked back and forth getting lost as one does in a maze, and as I shepherded him out, the thought came to me, 'I could leave him here and drive off.' I pictured the newspaper headline, 'Artist found lost in maze'.

Mum would be livid. If I told her that I had wished to push him out of the car she would have said, 'How could you think such murderous thoughts?' She must have had her own. She had more reason to than I did.

One Sunday I brought the camera with me, intending to take Dad's photograph, recalling the series of photographs that Richard Avedon took of his dying father. I stopped the car at a walking track. I took the camera out of the bag and slung it over my shoulder. 'I'll take the photo on the way back,' I said to myself. As we returned from the walk I paused before getting into the car. 'I have to do it now,' I thought. I turned and looked at my father. I stared at him, noting the position of the trees in the background, framing the photograph to ensure that a tree wasn't growing out of his head. My hand clung to the camera at my side, ready to raise it. I saw my father's bewildered confusion. I heard my mother's voice, 'How dare you.' To take the photograph would not only capture the image of his face but possibly also stir up a memory of the use of the camera. Dad posed cooperatively for photos, constructing himself for the photographer. The sight of the camera could elicit the thought that he had lost his former self. To take the photograph would be to capture the moment his terror of this loss was ignited.

Driving back home, I recalled the impulse not to take the photograph. It was like taking a man into a secluded part of the country and taking a gun to his head. 'Is this what happens when you plan a murder?' I thought. When it comes to the point, you can't do it. The photo could only have been taken if I had been able to resist my mother's voice: 'How dare you.' It could only have been taken if I had not imagined the terror that taking the photograph would induce in a man who had lost his mind and was vaguely aware of the use of the camera.

Although the photo was not taken, I can now re-create in memory the photograph I did not take.

It is black and white. An old man is looking at the camera. His eyes are watery, vacant. He is looking at the photographer in dazed puzzlement. His skin is blotched, marked with little tributary veins. His mouth is closed but not quite closed as if he is about to speak. His hair is unkempt. Something is missing. There is no angst, no depression, no self-loathing, no struggling with himself. He is not self-consciously posing for the photo, aware of the relationship to the photographer. He is a ghost of himself.

I like to think that it was not my mother's voice, 'How dare you', that stopped me from taking a photograph of my father. It was compassion.

*

Whenever I saw Dad, I put my thoughts and feelings on hold. I deferred to him. I entered his territory, asking him questions about art. I was fearful of his criticism, but I also wished to protect him. Deeply within him one sensed a vulnerability, a fragility, a void. It felt to me that a sense of dark precariousness hung over the family, exuding an ominousness that could never be referred to. I was not aware of it until I left home. I knew very little about Dad's childhood. I knew that he was estranged from his parents and that they lived not far from us. I didn't know their names. I knew that they had to leave school at twelve and thirteen as *their* parents could not afford to keep them at school. On the rare times Dad spoke of them, he emphasised that it wasn't their fault they didn't have an education.

Twice in my life I had occasion to refer to his parents. The first time I was sixteen. The phone rang soon after I got home from school.

'Is John there?'

'No, I am sorry he's not. Can I give him a message?'

'Tell him his mother rang.'

'Yes, I will Mrs Brack.'

She hung up. Moments later, I realised I had been speaking to my grandmother. Something had given me the presence of mind to politely call her 'Mrs Brack'. I remember preparing myself to tell my father, as if nervously going to speak to the headmaster. I waited until he was sitting alone in the sitting room. I went in.

'Daddy, your mother rang.' His head fell. 'She would like you to ring her.'

'Mmph,' he mumbled, looking at the floor. I tiptoed out. Message received.

We never spoke of Dad's parents. We never thought of them. It was as if they existed in some other place. When Mum matter-of-factly told me that Dad's father had died, I wanted Dad to know that I knew his father had died. *He* was *my* father. He must have felt something about the death of his father. I had to consider how to tell him. I could not say, 'I know your father has died.' That would sound accusing. I felt a pang of nervousness as I heard myself saying respectfully, 'Daddy, I am sorry to hear that your father died.' His head fell, his eyes looked down at the table. Silence. I refused to break the silence. 'Hmph,' he grunted. I had done something more invasive than knocking on the door of the studio and interrupting the important man. I had crossed the threshold of what was permissible to speak.

I had never seen a photograph of Dad's parents until the gathering after his funeral. It was then that Uncle Lindsay gave me three photographs—a photo of Dad as a young man, a photo of their father and a photo of their mother sitting on a seat with her two sons. In the photo with their mother, Dad looks about ten. Lindsay would be eight. Dad's head is inclined towards his mother, his arm around her back. His mother's head is inclined towards him. Lindsay sits on the other side of his mother, sitting straight up looking at the camera. I like to believe there was a time when Dad loved his mother and she loved him. The evidence is there in the photograph. The son's arm around his mother's back, their heads inclined towards each other.

The thought came to me: what if my father could find the love that I saw in that photograph of the boy with his mother? What if he made some connection with his parents? What if Dad *did* put down his paintbrush 'having said all that he wanted to say'? What if he stopped drinking? What if he didn't get dementia? What if he had an alternative ending to his life?

An alcoholic friend of my father's had fallen into the gutter after an afternoon and evening drinking in a pub. He was found by a passer-by and taken to hospital and then sent to another hospital to dry out. He went to AA and resurrected his career, avoiding the dementia that would have been his fate had he continued drinking.

What if I 'gave' this story to my father?

I could not imagine my father having a lover, but I could imagine him falling into the gutter, drunk. I could imagine him agreeing to stop drinking under the threat that if he didn't, he would get dementia. I could not imagine him sitting in a room with strangers talking about their drinking in meetings of AA. If he were to give up the grog, I would need to find an alternative to AA. Drinking was not a hobby. It was self-medication, an attempt at dealing with the torment of his life. I would have to find some other means for understanding what troubled him.

*

Something had troubled me.

For several months every night I woke up recalling a conflict with my boss. Night after night I replayed what he had said, what I had said, what he had said, how he had tricked me into agreeing to a meeting where he humiliated me in front of my colleagues.

I went to see a psychotherapist.

Instead of telling her what had happened with my boss I found myself telling her about an incident with my father.

'My father has dementia. He was in hospital having a prostate operation. He thought he was in a hotel. When I visited him, he had his back to me, washing his hands.

'"Hello Daddy," I said.

'He turned his face towards me, beaming. "I'm so glad to see you."

'He had never said he was glad to see me.

'"I'm so glad you're here. I didn't know how I could get home. I haven't got any money for a taxi. I thought I could ring Freda and ask her for some money, but I couldn't do that. It would be *abject*. It is *abject* for a parent to ask a child for money."

'I wanted my father to be pleased to see me.

'If it is abject for a parent to ask a child for money, it is even more abject for a father to lose his mind, especially a man known for his intelligence. "I am a cerebral painter," he said when asked what sort of painter he was. If I had been humiliated by the meeting called by my boss, he would have been even more humiliated had he known that he had lost his mind to dementia. Clambering for the dignity of his former self, he told me and the nurse taking his blood pressure, "See that hand-basin over there. I made that. I won first prize in a competition."

In the sessions with the psychotherapist, I discovered what had haunted me about the incident with my boss.

I began to wonder what would happen if my father went to see a psychotherapist. A therapist would provide the space to explore the self that required the self-medication. Dad preferred the intimacy of conversation with one trusted friend. It was beyond my suspension of disbelief to imagine him visiting a lover in the country, but faced with the choice between getting dementia and seeing a therapist, I imagine he would choose the therapist if there was no option to take his own life.

His sessions with a therapist would give me the opportunity to understand the origin of his torment. It would give me the opportunity to find compassion for him and for him to find compassion for himself.

If I were to write his sessions with a psychotherapist, I would have to overcome my mother's voice in me: 'Private is private'. In wondering about the notion of the private becoming public I recalled an exchange between two characters in a novel by Patrick White. The man has received 'a highly coloured post-card' with 'snatches of information'. The woman has received a poem about a glacier. The man asks to read the poem. The woman replies, 'It's far too private, I mean, you only show your poem to those you want to see it—unless, of course, you throw it wide open to the public.'

In throwing *this* wide open to the public, I draw on what my father has said in interview and conversation, what he has written and what I see looking at his paintings.

In his visits to the therapist Dad will speak about the person most important to him, the person on whom he depended: his wife. The reader will be introduced to my mother through the eyes of my father. In devising a scenario where my mother also speaks to a therapist, I explore the origin of her fear of what would emerge if the private was made known. I explore the relationship between her life and her paintings and her position in the world where the artist was assumed to be a man. In speaking to her therapist about Dad, the reader will gain an insight into her relationship to him and how she ensured that his work took priority.

The title of the book, *The Secret Landscapes*, refers to the secrets of my father's childhood. It refers to the secrets of my mother and those passed on from her parents. Secrets take the form of inner landscapes. Through confronting my own impulse to secrecy I explore how secrecy infiltrates the works of the writer and the artist. The subtitle, *On Not Pleasing Your Mother*, is from Janet Malcolm, who suggests that art is subversive, challenging the boundaries of what is permissible: 'Art is theft, art is armed robbery, art is not pleasing your mother'. My father defied his mother in choosing to be an artist, my mother defied her mother in her marriage to an artist, and in writing what my mother considered private I am defying her. In doing so I offer what she yearned for.

In earlier drafts, overshadowed by my mother's voice, 'private is private', Dad refers to Mum as 'Hilda'. In emerging from the shadow of the private, I gave my mother her real name. I refer to my father as 'Dad' although I never called him 'Dad', I called him 'Daddy'. Mum tells me that he called his parents 'Mother' and 'Pater'. She referred to them as 'Mr and Mrs Brack'.

I have called the therapists T and V as if they are real people wishing to maintain their anonymity.

Sessions with T

How would I actually get Dad to the sessions with the psychotherapist? Mum would have to drive him. On the way there he says, 'I don't know why I am going to see this fellow. I haven't done anything wrong.'

Mum: Look, it has been so much effort getting you off the grog. If you don't go, you will lose your mind with dementia. Do you want that? No. Well, I certainly don't. I don't fancy giving up my time to look after you.

Dad: I don't want to go.

Mum: You have to go and you have to do what the man says. And you have to say thank you when he's finished with you.

Dad: *(sarcastically)* Thank you, thank you, thank you.

He sits in the waiting room and then T arrives.

T: Welcome, John, come in. T indicates a chair.

As he sits down, Dad says: I'm only here because Helen says I have to be here. Apparently, you are rescuing me from dementia. Man to the rescue.

T: I am here to help you with what troubles you.

What troubles me goes into my paintings.

Long silence.

T: Just say whatever comes into your mind.

I am not the master of spontaneity. I am not the sort of artist who wakes up in the middle of the night declaring, 'I'll paint the moonlight.'

T: You are not here as an artist, you are here as a human being, a troubled human being.

My troubles go into my paintings. That's where they're hidden, if you care to find them.

T: It is said that 'the artist is like a child playing a sophisticated game of hide and seek. It is a joy to be hidden but a disaster not to be found.'

It is not a joy to be hidden, it is a necessity.

T: It is our work to take you out of hiding.

What do you mean *our* work? I've never worked with anyone in my life. The artist is a solitary being.

The statement, 'a joy to be hidden…' is from Donald Winnicott, a psychoanalyst. I am not pretending to be a psychoanalyst. The character of T is a literary device to explore the hidden life of my father.

For the next six months Dad sits in silence for the duration of the fifty minutes. T will make a brief comment at the beginning and the end of each session. Eventually Dad will say to T what he said to me during one of our drives in the country:

When I came home late from school, my mother hit me with my father's belt. She said it was for playing with the lower-class boys in the next street. I didn't know what I had done wrong. I thought we were lower class.

T: Are you telling me that you don't know what you have done wrong having to be here?

I don't know what I have done wrong. Every day I find myself retracing the steps of how I got to be here.

T: Tell me how you got to be here.

One morning Helen told me that she was going away to stay with her sister Emily for a few days. Her sister lived in the country. That evening, I came into the kitchen to heat up the dinner she had left for me but when I turned on the light a paralysing melancholy came over me. The simple act of turning on the light reminded me that Helen was not home. She usually set the table which meant that even getting the knife and fork felt onerous to me. I barely managed to eat the dinner she had cooked and then, after washing the plate, I poured myself more whiskey and stumbled into the sitting room where I turned on the television. I must have dozed off. I remember waking, fearful that something had happened to Helen and she would never return. I worried about not having enough whiskey in the house despite knowing a bottle was concealed under the leaves surrounding the bay tree.

I got up and walked out of the house towards the bottle shop, fully aware that the shop would be closed. I can only imagine that my wires had got crossed and in my deranged panic I thought that if the bottle shop was open Helen would return. I arrived at the darkened shop, knowingly defeated. Each step on returning home brought me closer to the emptiness of the house, to the despair that there would be nothing more to paint, to the worry that my memory was failing me.

As I stepped from the footpath onto the road, I tripped headlong into the gutter. Instinctively, I thrust out my arm to protect me but as I landed on the concrete, a fierce spasm of pain wracked through my arm. I had no will to get up. There was nothing I could do but succumb to lying sprawled where I had tripped. In silent resignation I closed my eyes like a child who imagines that if he closes his eyes no one can see him.

Here I am at the still point of the turning world, I said to myself. For the first time in my life, I had no fear of falling, no sense that something would topple over. I had fallen.

So this is it! I said to myself, as a man might declare gazing at the view from the summit of the mountain he had climbed. So this is it, the still point of the turning world. I found myself dozing in and out of sleep beyond caring what would happen to me.

I woke startled by a man's voice saying, 'My God, what's happened to you, mate?'

The voice was unfamiliar but then after a slap on the face I heard, 'Wake up. Wake up.'

Obediently I opened one eye and then closed it.

'Blood shot,' the man said, offering his layman's diagnosis. 'I'll get an ambulance. What's your name, mate?'

'Blood Shot,' I mumbled.

Were it not for the stranger who found me, I may never have arrived at the hospital. I would never have been told to stop drinking.

T: And now you are here.

And now I am here.

As I wrote that account, I could almost convince myself that Dad had fallen in the gutter and was rescued by a passer-by. I was giving my father an alternative ending to his life. He was coming alive on the page in dialogue with T. I was speaking as a ventriloquist in the voice of my father.

*

In the next session he says:

Mother's quest for me and my younger brother Lindsay was to get out of the working class. I knew that if we were to enter the middle class, we would have to do something about our accents which would give us away. Every day for three months Lindsay and I listened to the wireless and practised speaking in the voice of the ABC radio announcers who, in those days, spoke in the accent of the upper-class British man. There! I have told you something about myself. Twenty years after Mother hit me for playing with the lower-class boys in the next street, I married an upper-class girl from the other side of the river.

Mum would never have married Dad if he had not taught himself to speak in the accent of the ABC radio announcers. She told me about an exhibition opening. 'And there was [name of artist] speaking in that dreadful working-class accent. There he was going yob yob yob.'

He says to T:

No one knows the effort for the child of working-class parents to invent himself as a middle-class man.

T: Do you want to tell me the effort?

I want to tell you how I studied what was specifically required of the artist in Australia in the twentieth century. No artist is truly original. The evolution of any artist's work is very largely a recapitulation of the art of the past. One learns how to paint by studying the great masters and as the artist moves slowly and painfully towards finding his own schema, he becomes aware that each of his paintings could be titled 'Homage to...' I came to the discovery that if I painted in the recognisable style of the European masters but took life in the Australian suburbs as the subject of the painting, the work would contribute to shaping our identity and therefore my own identity as an artist.

T: You are giving me insight into your work as an artist. Is this a gift I am privileged to receive or is this a means to distract us?

The artist is his work. I was in it for the long haul. And now the long haul is over.

T: The artist may well be his work. This is our work exploring the inner life of the man who constructed the persona of the middle-class man that demanded so much effort. We are in this for the long haul.

*

In the next session he tells T:

My father left school when he was twelve years old. It was the Depression. He worked in the brewery. Mother left school at thirteen and learnt to sew as a milliner and dressmaker. I have one brother, Lindsay, who is two years younger than I am.

Mother expected us to do very well at school, to 'pull the family out of poverty' as if 'poverty' was a well we had to be pulled out from. Mother had something more invested in me than simply earning a decent living. In her mind I was destined to be a genius. She expected great things from me. It pleased me to please her with my good marks. Mother's praise made me feel indestructible.

One of my earliest memories is of Mother taking me and Lindsay to the toy shop to select the present from Father Christmas. My eyes fell on a model of a German howitzer gun. I knew that it cost more than Mother could afford and therefore beyond what we were permitted. I looked at it avidly, picked it up and studied how it worked while Lindsay contented himself with looking at the lead soldiers within Mother's price range.

On Christmas day it delighted me to see that Father Christmas had given me the toy I had found irresistible. In compensation that Lindsay had not received such an exotic toy, I allowed him to play with it whenever he wanted. I once carved him a realistic automatic pistol from a solid piece of wood.

T: You are telling me that you discovered that your mother would make concessions to you that she did not make for your brother.

There were other concessions. She had taken us to buy new coats which she had heard were on special. When we arrived at the shop, she veered us towards a table tumbling with coats. She poked her hand into the thriving mass and extracted a coat which she held against me. The dull purple left me aghast. I refused to try it on leaving Mother to persuade Lindsay to try on the coat she had selected while I looked at a rack of garments not marked down on special.

Lindsay and I walked out wearing our new acquisitions, he resigned to the indignity of purple and me in respectable navy blue. On the way home we called in to visit Aunty Ethel. Mother explained we had been shopping for new coats. Aunty Ethel looked at each of us appraisingly, 'What good taste John has,' she said.

T: You discovered that your mother made sacrifices for you.

As I said, Mother saw me as special. I remember my embarrassment when I overheard her reading out my report card to Aunty Ivy. 'They're just marks. What's all the fuss?' Aunty Ivy said, refusing to respond as was expected of her. It was then that I knew that the good marks were for Mother. Mother was claiming my 'success' as her own. It was like the shock of discovering that your mother isn't really your mother, she is someone else.

Mother's anger when I said I wanted to go to the art school confirmed that her praise was only forthcoming if I did what was expected of me. It wasn't my success she wanted. She wanted my success for herself. I wanted to tell her, 'We have to be separate. A mother can't live through her son. You have to find your own meaning in life.'

T: It was a wound for both of you when the honeymoon was over.

I doubt that T would say that, but that is the sentence that wrote itself.

If Mother saw me as special, Pater saw me as his accomplice. He would take me by the hand and say, 'Let's ask Mother, shall we.' He liked to keep the peace. He was easily intimidated. It wasn't his fault he had to leave school at twelve years old.

I remember the moment I realised my father's inadequacy. I was ten years old. He had taken me and Lindsay to the museum on Sunday afternoon. As we huddled over the exhibits, my father read aloud the sign next to the glass cabinet, even though we were capable of reading it ourselves. I stood idly looking on, distracted by another father at the neighbouring exhibit. The other father was not reading the sign, he was explaining the exhibit in his own words, responding to the questions his children asked, elaborating.

As we waited at the bus stop, Pater attempted to engage me in conversation, reporting a fact about one of the exhibits we had seen. He had confused one exhibit with another. Fuelled by my disappointment in him, I did something I had never done before.

'No, you're wrong,' I said. 'Don't you know that? Don't you know anything?'

My father raised his hand as if shielding his eyes from the sun. He may have intended to slap me but then thought the better of it. As his hand covered his eyes, the shame of my father burned through me. My brother witnessed the little fire knowing it was I who had lit the match.

T: You had humiliated your father for not being the sort of father you would have liked.

And you are not the sort of psychotherapist I would have liked. There must be others better than you. I don't even know who you are. I know nothing about you. Helen's father was a psychiatrist. Before coming to see you I'd never even heard of a 'psychotherapist'. Besides, how can any of us understand another person, let alone ourselves?

T: We are all ordinary human beings. We are all mortal, the Nobel Prize winner, the cashier in the supermarket, the man who collects the tickets on the tram. We are all interconnected. We are all connected to the trees, the stars, the animals of this world. If we look at it this way our hearts can be healed.

What makes you think that little statement will make any difference to me?

T: A little statement like a poem or a painting can wait for us. It is there to recall when we are receptive to it.

What is the point of any of this? I give up. I am leaving.

He leaves before the end of the session.

If Dad didn't want to hear something, he would get up and walk out of the room, supposedly to get more whiskey and more ice. You would hear the iceblocks being extracted from the aluminium iceblock tray, and then the occasional cursing as the iceblocks danced onto the floor.

*

In the next session he says:

You are right. I had humiliated my father for not being the sort of father I would have liked. I was probably not the sort of son that he would have liked.

Inadvertently I once humiliated Mother. I had got a scholarship to Ivanhoe Grammar. A school uniform was required. As I tried on the jumper, the blazer and the long pants, Mother looked on admiringly. Uniforms impressed her. She had been led to believe that the school would pay for the uniform as part of the scholarship. This proved not to be the case. She could not afford to pay for the uniform. The source of her hope and pride was now the source of her profound disappointment. I had done my part in getting the scholarship to go to the private school. She had not done her part in buying the uniform to go there. I could not take up the scholarship.

T: You felt you had inadvertently humiliated your mother.

It wasn't my fault, but I felt protective of Mother. I did not blame her that I could not take up the scholarship. She was more disappointed than I was.

After I left school at fifteen and a half, I got a job in an insurance office in the city. If it were not for a chance encounter one day after work, I may never have become an artist. I was passing a shop in Little Collins Street when I saw amongst the clutter in the window two coloured reproductions of paintings by Van Gogh. I was overcome with shuddering and a shiver in the spine. The thought came to me, 'If painting could do that, I could do that.' The torment of the soul could express itself in something as mundane as a bed and a chair in the swirling of the paint.

T: It was an epiphany.

It was an epiphany. I will never forget that shudder of recognition. I had a purpose in life. The next year I enrolled in night classes at the gallery art school. A year later I saw for the first time an unfinished Cézanne landscape. Again, I was overcome by a shuddering, a tingling in the spine. The painting was speaking to me even more directly than the Van Gogh which I had only seen in reproduction. I knew something in that moment although I could not articulate what I knew. The painting had lifted me out of the drab suburban ordinariness of the 1930s. If Cézanne and Van Gogh could do that, I could do that.

I had to postpone my classes at the gallery school in 1940 when I turned twenty and enlisted in the army. The six years in the army provided no opportunity to paint or to have contact with other painters as the night classes had. In those years between twenty and twenty-five, the artist makes vital decisions based on how he interprets the work of his elders. He sees himself continuing a lineage based on his interpretation of what has come before. I never wanted to join an art movement. This may have been because I spent those formative years alone without contact with other artists. Fortunately, it suited my temperament not to belong.

T: So instead of bemoaning what you missed out on in those six years in the army, you saw what you had gained.

Exactly.

The time in the army was my first time away from home. My parents kept in touch through disappointing letters. It is not that I expected Dostoevsky. I could hardly complain about the inadequacy of their letters to me as my letters to them were no less mundane. I would mention a humorous little incident of no consequence whatsoever. It may have been my references to the promotions that led to Mother's conviction that she would eventually become the mother of a general in the army.

When I returned home after six years, I was no longer the naïve twenty-year-old youth who had thought of himself as a man. It was disconcerting to notice that the furniture in the house was arranged just as it was when I left. I sat in the same chair at the kitchen table. Mother was only interested in one thing: what I was going to 'do' in my life. When I told her I intended enrolling full time in the art school she responded with, 'What do you want to do that for?' She had hoped that my time in the army would rid me of my 'little hobby' and I would agree to the more reputable career she had in mind for me.

As I ate my dinner, I pictured myself getting up and leaving the table, the room, the house and never returning. I didn't know what I was doing there, and yet there was nowhere else to go. I knew I would have to keep living at home until I could earn enough money to pay the rent for a place of my own.

After dinner I sat on my bed and closed my eyes thinking, 'Everything is just the same. Everything is dead like a museum.' I wanted to shake some sense into Mother: 'A parent can't live through the child. Each of us must find our own meaning in life. Can't you get that into your fat head. Don't you understand. I want to be an artist.'

It wasn't Mother's fault she missed out on an education, but I do not know what stopped her from getting a job. She had trained as a milliner so there was nothing to stop her getting a job making her little hats. She was an expert at sewing dresses. That wasn't good enough for her. She wanted her son to be important, to do something in the world, not, as she saw it, getting out of proper work, dabbling with pencils and paints.

The next day I walked along the street churning with fury at Mother, wrestling with anger at my father for not defending me, castigating myself for having the audacity to hope that my parents would affirm what I wanted to do in my life. I kept walking with nowhere to go until I found myself walking through the open gates of the Kew cemetery. I made my way towards a gravestone, put my head in my hands and burst into tears. Where else is one permitted to weep but in a graveyard? I wept for the wretched pitifulness that everything was just the same. I wept for my own stupidity in having imagined that it would be different. I wept for the futility of the deaths I had witnessed in the army. I didn't care that Mother would see me as a sook. What did she know? She didn't know what had happened in the army.

T: You discovered that you could weep without admonishing yourself for 'being a sook', defying your mother.

And when I stood up, I felt that I had been restored to myself. In this newfound lightness of being I picked up a faded pink plastic carnation lying on the pathway and manoeuvred it into my buttonhole. When I arrived home just in time for dinner Mother asked me where I had been. 'I've been to a wedding. My own wedding. I'm married to a rainbow.'

Dad could not weep in the presence of his mother. I could not think in his presence.

'Did you see me in the newspaper?' I asked him, pointing to a photograph of hundreds of runners about to start a marathon. He had no interest in sport. At school you could either be good at sport or good at your work. We were expected to be good at our work.

'I ran twenty-five miles, forty-two kilometres.'

He looked at the photo. 'What did you want to do that for?'

It did not occur to me to say, 'Isn't that what your mother said when you told her you wanted to be an artist?'

I could not think in the presence of my father. He may have felt the same about being in the presence of his father and his mother.

*

He says to T:

My father was a defeated man. I, too, was defeated time and time again. I had originally wanted to be a poet, but my attempts at poetry had failed. Words would always defeat me. Years later when I read that Cézanne had said, 'I have failed to realise my sensations', I understood that the artist's sense of defeat does not necessarily arise from the limits of his talent, it arises in all artists and writers. One is always working at the limits of one's intelligence. The work never lives up to the ideal, the fantasy of its original conception.

Dad said he originally wanted to be a poet. He read a lot. He was very particular with words. When I visited for lunch with my four-year-old and two-year-old, he would place his *Oxford English Dictionary* on a chair, raising the height of the chair like a cushion. During lunch he would ask the four-year-old the meaning of 'obstreperous', 'dilapidated', 'euphemism'.

*

He says to T:

As an art student, on Sunday afternoons I looked at paintings in the art gallery. One late afternoon, I stepped out into the street overcome with a sense of dislocation as if my body had separated itself from me. I assumed it was my eyes adjusting to the sunlight away from the intensity of the paintings I had seen in the art gallery, but the feeling persisted until I arrived at a park. The autumn light cast shadows on the green lawn. Mothers, fathers and grandparents were walking with children. Single men and women were strolling alone. Couples reclined on the grass. Three or four boys were kicking a football. As I took in the scene, I found myself composing the tableau before me as a painting. The painting I constructed in my mind was an echo of Seurat's *A Sunday Afternoon on the Island of La Grand Jatte*.

The people in Seurat's painting were more grandly dressed. The ladies were holding parasols, but the effect was the same. They were *enjoying* themselves on Sunday afternoon. They were 'at leisure'. They were together as families. 'Leisure' sent me into moments of existential terror. There was something I should be doing. I should be painting. I have never longed for a 'pleasant' Sunday afternoon walking in the park, strolling with the family. I needed the solitude to think about painting, keeping a connection to the current work if I was not in the studio working.

T: You are telling me that painting did something with the existential terror that you should be *doing* something.

I should be doing something now. I should be painting. I don't know why I am here. Why am I telling you this? I don't know anything about you. For all I know, you could have poisoned your mother and thrown her down the well. Look at you with your Persian carpet, the books on the bookshelf, the fancy lampshade, the dark-green velvet chairs. You know nothing about poverty.

T: I cannot know your experience of poverty if you do not tell me what it is. I can only go on what you tell me.

*

In the next session he notices a vase of daffodils in T's room. At the sight of the daffodils, he recalls William Wordsworth's poem. He starts by saying:

I wandered lonely as a child
That floats on high o'er vales and hills,
When all at once I saw a crowd,
A host, of golden daffodils;
Beside the lake, beneath the trees,
Fluttering and dancing in the breeze.

T: Did you hear what you just said?

I wandered lonely as a cloud that floats…

T: You said, 'I wandered lonely as a child.' Were you a lonely child?

I had no friends. There was no other boy I was drawn to and if any boy made a move to befriend me, I was ignorant of the move. I was wandering in my childhood. I had no idea of what I wanted to do in my life. I just knew I did not want to do what my father did.

T: You had no friends.

I will always remember meeting the man who would become my first friend. I was twenty when I went into the army. As I removed my books out of my bag, a hand grabbed one of them and a voice declared 'books', as if it was my teddy bear I had brought with me.

'Look what he's got. Books.' The pages were being flipped when I heard another voice declaring, 'Poetry!!'

I dared not look up and face my accusers. I feared the precious books would be ripped into shreds. Then I heard a voice saying, 'Give them to me.' I looked up and to my astonishment the men relinquished the books. And so it was that in an army camp in Greta, New South Wales, I met John Stephens, my first friend.

T: This man rescued you from your initiation into the army.

He rescued me. I remember the first time we discussed Rilke's *Letters to a Young Poet*. I had considered novels and poetry a solace, but not something you could talk to with another human being. Stephens had been to university. He could converse about ideas, about literature, about novels.

When Stephens returned from the army, he worked as a stockbroker in the city, but he suffered terrible guilt. Something had happened in the army. His boss sent him to see 'the best psychiatrist in Melbourne' who, as Helen liked to remind me, was none other than her father. He married Joan and embarked on writing a novel which did not come to fruition. He and Joan left Melbourne and bought a farm in Mittagong, New South Wales. Over the years, a tension emerged between us. I attributed this tension to the gap between my increasing success and

Stephens' failure to live up to his promise. It was Stephens who had come to my rescue that first night in the army. It was Stephens who had given me the benefits of his university education.

T: It was Stephens who had shown you the possibilities of friendship. What stopped you from speaking to me about Stephens before this?

I don't know. You tell me!

T: Stephens had come to your rescue in that humiliating initiation into the army. I had come to your rescue from losing your mind with dementia. If Stephens could fall apart, who is to say that I would not fall apart? If 'the best psychiatrist in Melbourne' could not help Stephens, how could you trust that I would have any luck with you?

Dad's last letters to John Stephens have been put into the National Library. They comment on the difficulties of painting, the deadline for an exhibition, the negotiations with a gallery director. They end with 'give my love to Joan'. I do not recall Dad being especially fond of Joan. It may have been Stephens that he wanted to give his love to.

*

In the next session he says:

I was able to enrol full time at the National Gallery art school under a grant from the Commonwealth Rehabilitation Scheme. I was seven years older than most of the other students who had come straight from school. Unlike them, I had no time to waste. When they chatted in the breaks and at lunch time, I kept to myself.

One lunch time I was walking along the street when I noticed two of the girl students coming towards me; one was a giggling dill and the other a more studious girl who stayed back for the night class. As they passed, the dill clumsily made faces while the other looked embarrassed. I ignored them.

Late that afternoon I was working on a drawing before the night class. Nobody else was around. I heard the door to the studio open and then looked up to see the embarrassed girl coming towards me. Without any introduction she said excitedly, 'Did you know that Seurat used the same technique that we are being taught?'

I didn't know where she'd got that idea. 'No he didn't,' I said. 'Seurat only used the pointillist technique.'

She showed me the book. I had to admit she was right. Then, without thinking, I heard myself suggest we have dinner before the night class the next week. A week later I arrived where we had planned to meet, surprised to see that she was not alone. She was chatting to the student I had seen assiduously sketching in the portrait class. Freddy would be joining us for dinner. I thought he may have been her boyfriend, but when it became apparent that he wasn't, I was reassured.

I recalled the first time I had seen Freddy. One gloomy afternoon at the gallery school I was doing a pastiche of Leonardo da Vinci when I glanced up to see a young man entering the studio holding an armful of paper. He sat down and rapidly set about covering each sheet with charcoal studies of the head of the model we were drawing. After a few minutes, each sheet of paper turned into a black cloud which he then tossed impatiently onto the floor. What struck me instinctively was that while all of these studies failed to accomplish what I could see he was aiming for, the attitude and the determination were those of the first real artist I had ever encountered.

When I realised he would be joining Helen on our first outing, I was secretly overjoyed. A few months later Freddy confessed that when Helen told him she was having dinner with 'that older rehab student who keeps to himself' he suggested coming along as a chaperone. For the same reason I had wanted to meet him, he had wanted to meet me.

Freddy and I shared a studio near the gallery school. We put a bed in the studio so we could take shifts sleeping. It was our way of living away from home. Although we were personally compatible, Freddy's painting technique was somewhat different from my own. In his eagerness to get at the paint, tubes of paint were simply chopped in half. His painting procedure was frenetic. Frequently when the brush seemed too slow, the paint was applied impatiently, often desperately, with a rag. Despite this, we had a similar approach to our work. Each of us felt the alienation of the artist but neither of us stooped to the bohemianism expected of an artist.

It was only once in my life that I ever felt cross with Freddy. I was meeting Helen for lunch. She had asked me to bring the petticoat she had left in the studio. I was about to give up looking when a splash of pale pink caught my eye near Freddy's paintbrushes. I grabbed it, knowing instantly what had happened. Freddy had used it to wipe his paintbrushes. I would have done the same thing had I not recognised the pink lying on the floor as a petticoat. It was Freddy who had ruined it but, even so, I anticipated Helen's anger.

'Good Lord,' she said, examining the defaced garment I had returned. 'That's just Freddy. He wouldn't have a clue. Mum bought that for me at Georges.' In other words, it was expensive.

As I walked back to the studio, it occurred to me how easily I had anticipated the anger of a woman. It was Mother's voice. It was Mother's voice in me I could not escape.

T: It is our work together to understand this.

What do you mean, 'our work together'? It's not as if we are building a sandcastle.

T: It is not just work we are doing. Maybe we are playing. Maybe we are making something together, something with the splendour of a castle.

*

The next session he says:

I painted two portraits of Freddy. He painted two of me. I was a more experienced portrait painter so his portraits of me were not as accomplished as mine. It was a mark of our friendship that he was prepared to do my portrait on both occasions.

He struggled and struggled with the first portrait in 1950 until the canvas was encrusted with so many layers of paint it could almost stand up by itself. I do not know the fate of this struggle. Thirty years later he did another portrait of me. I am sitting on a chair in a jacket and a tie, ruddy faced, scowling, eyes averted, hands on my knees, maintaining what little dignity I have. Darkness surrounds me. Freddy did not romanticise the troubled artist. He did not pretty up the image of a friend. He saw the decrepitude I made no pretence to conceal.

T: You allowed Freddy to see you as you really are. You are allowing me to see you as you really are.

In 1948, at twenty-eight, Dad drew a self-portrait depicting the self-conscious promise of the artist as a young man. In 1955, at the age of thirty-five, he painted a self-portrait as a confident, self-assured man. In 1972, at the age of fifty-two, he painted his body reflected in a shop window, outside looking in. It is not a self-portrait but it is the closest image of himself after painting the self-portraits. His head is concealed in the darkness of a shadow.

*

In the next session he says:

When Helen showed me the book on Seurat, she was just one of the girl students who had come straight from school. I knew very little about girls. I had met Yvonne Lenny in the night class before going into the army and vaguely imagined that I might marry her until she told me she was marrying a 'real artist'. The real artist was Arthur Boyd who came from a 'real artist' family. Briefly, I corresponded with Ruth who I met before joining the army, but apart from that, my knowledge of women was non-existent.

Helen's upbringing could not have been more different than my own. At fifteen I had left school to get a job to earn money. At fifteen, Helen was at St Catherine's private school with one tutor teaching her art and others teaching her the piano and the flute. She wanted to leave school to go to the art school, but her father insisted she stay to finish school. He then paid the art school fees as well as the fees for the conservatorium where she studied the flute. Before the war, the Maudsley household was maintained by a cook, housekeeper, nurse, nannies and a governess.

When Helen told me she was pregnant, it seemed inevitable that we would live together, but given that her parents would never approve of us living together, one afternoon I found myself in Christ Church, South Yarra, signing the marriage certificate with Helen's parents, my parents, Stephens and one or two friends.

T: You had to get married for the approval of Helen's parents.

Not only that, after my marriage to Helen, I discovered that it was obligatory to attend the Christmas afternoon tea at the home of her Aunt Cecil. As we approached the imposing brick mansion, it seemed to me we were entering another country.

We entered the dining room, confronted by a large oval table draped in a white tablecloth covered with an array of scones, sandwiches and cakes. I seated myself next to Helen as far from the head of the table as permissible. A woman wearing an extraordinary hat introduced herself as Nancy Adams. Her eccentricity seemed the only thing out of place, apart from myself, and I was thankful for her exuberant chatter which meant that nothing was required of me except to listen.

As I glanced around the table, I thought I recognised an elderly gentleman sitting next to Emily, Helen's sister. In that disconcerting space between recognising someone and not knowing where one has met them, I half-heartedly listened to Mrs Adams, wondering where I had seen this man before. It wasn't the army. It wasn't the art school. Then I was struck with a moment of recognition. His photograph was hanging in the lobby of the insurance office where I worked after leaving school. It was L.F. Miller, the managing director. Nobody in my department had ever set eyes on L.F. Miller. I could not understand what he was doing sitting at the same table as I was. What was he doing there? A figure from my past, albeit in a framed photograph, had been inserted into what was already a discomfiting scenario. No one else seemed to notice the incongruity. I remember manoeuvring a chocolate éclair around the plate like a toy car, wondering how he got to be there. In what felt like an emergency, I could not put up my hand and ask permission to leave the room. The thought of making an escape reminded me that we would be required to perform the tedious ritual of shaking hands again before leaving.

Immediately we were out of earshot I asked Helen, 'What was L.F. Miller doing there?'

'He's my uncle.'

'What was he doing there?' I asked again.

'He's my uncle, Uncle Leo.'

I repeated the question, 'But what was he doing there?'

It took an effort of imagination to think of 'L.F. Miller' as the same person as 'Uncle Leo'.

T: Could it be that in repeating the question, 'What was L.F. Miller doing there?' you were asking yourself the question, 'What was I doing there?'

I am asking myself the question, 'What am I doing *here*?' I should be in the studio painting.

*

The next session he tells T:

The afternoon tea at the home of Helen's aunt was followed by the ordeal of the Maudsley family Christmas dinner. Helen and I were the youngest people there. The others were the medical friends of Helen's father. I remember sitting down at the long dining room table as the other guests found their places; unlike me, familiar with the ritual. The crisp white tablecloth had a decorousness lacking in the gingham cloth we had at home. For something to do I picked up the circular silver napkin holder and noticed that it was engraved with someone's initials, presumably Helen's family. The formal magnificence unnerved me. I remember playing with a little sprig of holly, poking the prickled edges into my hand in a private flagellation.

During the dinner, the woman next to me asked the question I should have anticipated, 'What do you do, John?' Her response was predictable. 'I've never met an artist before!' I felt like a rare species longing to escape to his own territory.

After the plum pudding the guests all stood up simultaneously. I began to follow Helen but my relief at departure was short-lived. It seemed that the women adjourned to the sitting room while the men remained at the dining room table. Gloomily I returned to my chair, discouraged at the prospect of what was to follow. Gathering my senses, I succumbed to the port as the gentlemen launched into talking about the Great War as if picking up where they had left off from the last Christmas. I noticed Helen's father going to the sideboard collecting the remaining knives, forks and spoons which he then placed on the table. The gentlemen then picked up these various knives, forks and spoons and used them to represent armies, replaying the battles from the Great War. I could imagine no greater discrepancy between life in the trenches and sitting drinking port in this grand mansion in South Yarra.

*

Dad called Mum's father 'Sir'. I called him 'Fafa', an abbreviation of grandfather. Every Saturday one of us children accompanied Mum to the Prahran market. We took the tram to her mother's house and then Granny would drive us to the market in her car. We arrived at Mum's parents' house as they were finishing breakfast. I remember one morning coming into the dining room and seeing the silver tureens of stewed fruit, little silver toast rack, white table napkins. Fafa was sitting at the head of the table. He didn't say hello as he usually did. He sat there, his head lowered.

I give this experience to my father:

As we got in the taxi to leave the Christmas dinner, I remembered that I had left my jacket hanging over the back of the dining room chair. I sprinted up the Punt Road hill back to the house I had enthusiastically left moments before. I knocked on the door which was opened by Helen's mother, who regarded me with her usual suspicion.

'I've left my jacket,' I said, intending to slip into the dining room unnoticed. I stood in the doorway and looked in. Cigar and cigarette smoke swirled towards the high ceiling. The room was lit from the candles that continued to flicker in the silver candelabra. I was about to make a move to collect my jacket when I noticed a figure concealed in the semi darkness. Helen's father sat alone, vacantly staring at the knives and forks that had collapsed after the battle re-enactments. He looked up in the realisation of one who has been discovered, taken off guard. He gave no sign of composing himself for an observer. No words were spoken between us as I collected my jacket and left the room. I recall a dark-red velvet curtain hanging over the window, a backdrop to the smoky haziness in the candlelight, the man alone deep in contemplation. The scene bore the emotional resonance of a Rembrandt painting.

T: What was the significance of this scene?

He knew and I knew in that moment that we both suffered from depression.

T: You had an affinity with your father-in-law that required no words.

I must have passed a test for shortly after the Christmas dinner I was offered a job as the art master at Melbourne Grammar. I had no teaching qualifications. I had not done the fifth or the sixth form. I understood that Dr Maudsley was friends with the headmaster who was also a member of the Melbourne Club. Although not having applied for the job, I happily accepted as it was more lucrative than framing pictures and as it was only two days and two evenings a week, there was sufficient time for painting.

Dr Maudsley offered me another invitation, this time to join the Melbourne Club. In order to please him I found myself agreeing to go along to be introduced. Nothing could have been more alienating for me. I should not have put myself through this ordeal. The next day I wrote a short, polite note declining the invitation.

Many years later we were called to Helen's parents' house, where her father lay dying. Helen was ushered upstairs into the bedroom where Emily and a few close friends had gathered while I was shown into the sitting room downstairs, wondering what was expected of me. Under the circumstances it did not seem appropriate to sit down and make myself at home, so I stood staring at a painting by Rupert Bunny. I then gazed out the window, wondering if I had been forgotten or if I was supposed to be somewhere else. Just as I was wondering what to do next, I heard the door opening. I turned and Helen came into the room. 'Dad died,' she said.

I burst into tears.

T: You felt grief for this man who understood you.

I never told him what he meant to me. He is there in *Collins St 5pm*. He is there indirectly in my magnum opus *The Battle*, a painting of the Battle of Waterloo. The pens and pencils that represent armies take their origin from the knives and forks of the battle re-enactments on Christmas day.

*

After the death of Mum's parents, the Christmas dinner was held at our family home. Mum would spend two weeks tidying the house, shopping and cooking for the dinner, trying out recipes, making Christmas cards and shopping for presents for the grandchildren. Dad's only task was to pour the wine and carve the meat. He would invariably pick up the carving knife and fork, slice a piece of meat and declare, 'The meat is overcooked.' It could be undercooked. His contribution to the dinner conversation was to respond to questions about art.

After dinner, several of us cleared up and washed the dishes. One year I was standing alone washing the last of the dishes when I heard a clearing of the throat. I looked up to see Dad standing in the doorway.

'You're too thin,' he said.

A surge of disgust arose from deep within me. No words would come. I wanted to say, 'Look at you, an overweight, unfit, blotchy red-faced man. What have you done to contribute to Christmas? You have not done a thing.' He had *invited* my disgust.

Mum tells the story of a time early in their marriage.

'Ursula had come to dinner. Ursula and John were talking about Thomas Mann's *The Magic Mountain*. I was listening to the conversation when I heard a reference to Beethoven's Piano Sonata No. 32, Op. 111.

'"I know that piece," I said.

'Straight away John replied, "No, you don't. You wouldn't know anything about Beethoven."

'"I'm sorry John," I said. "You're mistaken. I *do* know that piece of music."

'"Don't be ridiculous," he said. "What would you know?"

'"I do know that piece," I said. "I know that piece off by heart. I played it in one of my music exams."

'John still did not believe me. Ursula believed me. John thought he had married a silly little girl. He had no idea.'

'What would you know? You dope.'

'You fathead. Don't you know anything? Don't they teach you anything at school/university?'

I used to think Dad's remarks were about me or Mum or whichever one of us he was addressing. He was the father, the man in authority. Now I know he was telling us about himself. He was telling us of his own self-loathing.

I had imagined tipping my father out of the car, leaving him to wander lost on the country road. I want to express my anger at him for how he undermined us. I want T to get him to see how he inflicted his self-loathing onto his wife and children and the damage he had done in doing so. It is not likely that he would report to T on his undermining of his wife and children. T could *conclude* this is how he spoke to his children from how he speaks to him.

*

In the next session he says to T:

Anyway, I don't know why I am here. You're supposed to be helping me but what would you know? You're only a psychotherapist or whatever. I don't even know what you are. Yes, I do know, you're a charlatan. You might think you know everything about me, but you don't. You don't know what I am not telling you. Ha ha ha. Who do you think you are? All life is a series of defeats. Each parent aims to correct the mistakes of their parents, but we never succeed. The artist works out his despair in his painting. I doubt that Goya saw anyone called a 'psychotherapist'. What good would it have done him? He might not have painted those magnificent, troubling works. Helen's father was a psychiatrist, but if *he* didn't have any luck with Stephens, how could *you* have any luck with me? I don't know why I am here. Man hands on misery to man, that is the human condition. There are no pills for melancholia, for existential angst, there are no words that would cure what deeply troubles us as human beings. You are not giving me an instruction manual, you hardly say a word, leaving me to do the talking. What use is that? What have you got to show for all your work, whatever it is? You could hardly call it 'work', sitting on a chair muttering a few words whenever you felt like it. At least an artist has his painting. What do you have to show for yourself? Nothing.

T: You are wallowing in your sense of yourself as a defeated man. You are relishing your despair. You seem to think your misery gives you deeper insight into the human condition than those superficial idiots who are capable of joy. You are not aware of the depths of your misogyny. None of us are. You nurture your self-loathing, dishing it out to others, undermining your wife and children, if it's anything like what you say to me. You are constantly finding fault, criticising other people's effort. You might be gifted with a certain sort of intelligence, you might be talented at painting, you might have painted some magnificent works, but ultimately you go to the grave like everybody else.

He gets up and leaves before the end of the session.

I want him to claim his self-loathing, to divest myself of its shadow.

*

The next session he says:

I remember an incident in my first year of teaching at Melbourne Grammar. A boy in the sixth form had refused to do what I asked so I told him to stay back after the other boys had left. He was slouching with disdain in this well-equipped art room, muttering, 'Art is stupid. Art is a waste of time. It doesn't lead anywhere. What use is art?' He was mouthing what I assumed were his parents' platitudes about art.

I grabbed the lapels of his expensive blazer with the embroidered motif and its Latin insignia. I dragged him towards the wall and banged his head against it. The sound of the head hitting the wall made me aware of the brutality I was inflicting on him. 'You don't realise how fortunate you are!' I said, hit hit hit against the wall. 'You are squandering your opportunities.' Hit hit. 'You know nothing. You know nothing! You dill, you idiot.'

Here he was, in this most prestigious of private schools, telling me that art is a waste of time. My parents could not afford the uniform to the minor private school which meant I could not take up the scholarship. I had not even got to the sixth form. I had to leave school to earn money.

I remember preparing my defence in the event that the boy reported the incident to his parents. His father may have been a lawyer, a barrister or a judge. As it happened, he gave me no further trouble. In fact, I remember praising him for his *Still Life of Apples and Oranges in the manner of Cézanne*.

T: In telling me that you were unprofessional in banging the boy's head against the wall in your frustration, you are telling me that I was unprofessional in giving you my tirade, such as it was.

I am telling you that I am now prepared to do the work, whatever that is.

*

In the next session, he says to T:

As I was walking down the street to come here, I felt a pang of anxiety at the sight of the director of the National Gallery walking towards me. I feared he would ask me where I was going. As he came closer, I realised it was someone else and then as I continued walking I remembered Mother hitting me with my father's belt for playing with the lower-class boys in the next street.

T: You felt ashamed of coming to see me. Your mother was ashamed of being lower class. She took out her resentment in hitting you with your father's belt.

You fathead. You don't know anything.

T: If the way you speak to me is anything like the way you spoke to your children, you were not literally hitting them, you were undermining them with 'fatheads', 'dills', 'dopes'. As you did not know why your mother hit you for playing with the lower-class boys, they would not have known that you were speaking of your own self-loathing.

They will have to work that out for themselves.

*

In the next session he says:

You may have noticed that I didn't retaliate when you referred to my self-loathing. It reassured me. It was as if you had always known and only then considered it the right time to tell me.

T: So we are getting somewhere. Congratulations.

I remember the first time I was asked to pretend to be someone I wasn't. I had given my first lecture on art. People in the audience were putting up their hands asking questions expecting me to know the answers as if I was some kind of expert. You appear to be someone who knows because of your position and yet you don't know. I felt like an impostor. I remember thinking, Who do you think you are? Who do you think you are pretending you know when you don't?

The same thing happened in the army. I was barely twenty-four years old when I became promoted above the other lads the same age as me. The men came to me with their problems, feeling inadequate for the tasks demanded of them, missing their mothers, worried about what they would do when they returned to civilian life. Some like me were experiencing their first time away from home. They imagined I didn't have the problems they had because of my position.

T: Perhaps you imagine that I have everything worked out, I don't have any problems. I am here totally for you.

Well, aren't you?

*

In the next session he says:

I have not told you about the scholarship painting, a painting I entered in the Travelling Scholarship prize. The scholarship was awarded on the submission of a major painting in the final year of the art school. The winner was given an allowance to travel overseas for six months to study the paintings of the great masters. I was determined to win the prize. I was older than most of the other students. I had read novels, philosophy and poetry. I had thought long and hard about the role of the Australian artist after the war, concluding that the artist must say something about the Australian identity but work within the tradition of the European masters. It was incumbent on the artist not to paint gum trees like Streeton and McCubbin, but to make a comment on the suburban landscape.

With this understanding of the role of the artist, I embarked on a painting of the beach at Mentone. I had studied Seurat's painting *A Sunday Afternoon on the Island of La Grand Jatte* and applied the same vision to the painting I would call *The Beach*.

I remember the elation at having solved the problems of the painting. I knew this would become a formative work in my career and that I would develop what I had learnt in the subsequent work. Winning the prize would launch my career as an artist and confirm that I had made the right decision to be an artist. It would indicate to Mother that

I had talent. It would allow me to travel overseas to see Rembrandt's painting *The Jewish Bride* which I had wanted to see in the original ever since seeing a reproduction of it.

For six months after the winner was announced I found myself replaying the moment the name was called out. When one expects to hear one's own name and hears the name of another, one naturally thinks, 'There must be some mistake. They have got it all wrong.' I didn't understand it. Without much effort I had always been near the top of the class of sixty students. I had won the scholarship to the private school.

My despondency was relieved every so often with bouts of fury for Professor Joe Burke, the head of the judging panel. Apart from Ursula Hoff, never again did I trust people at the university. Despite my distrust of the judges, I feared they were right. I feared that I was deluding myself in thinking I had talent. I feared that I would be better off doing something else. However, I knew deep within myself that the judges were wrong, and I would prove them wrong eventually.

Helen's trite efforts at consolation only exacerbated my disappointment. It suited her that I did not get the scholarship, not that she would admit it. If I had won, I would have travelled overseas for six months, leaving her at home with the new baby, feeling resentment at not visiting the galleries herself. While I knew she was right—'it is just a prize'—the depression overwhelmed me. I wanted to eradicate the experience to spite the judges and to spite myself.

'I might as well burn the wretched thing,' I said to Helen, as if burning the painting would destroy the evidence that it had ever existed.

'Don't you dare,' she replied as if I was threatening to cut off the electricity.

She saw the painting as partly hers. I realised then that she saw my career as also hers. We were in this together.

I know now that it wasn't that I had failed to win the scholarship prize. It was that I had been convinced that I would win it. It was hubris.

T: You have told me of your hubris after identifying your self-loathing.

What have I got to lose?

I remember what was referred to as 'the scholarship painting'. It's a beach scene looking from the water towards the shore. A woman in bathers is standing on the shoreline, protectively placing her hand on a child's head. Her skin is pale to bright pink. A young, spindly man is drying his hair with a striped towel; a woman in black is sitting in what seems like a reverie; a man in a hat and a suit is standing on the beach, just looking. I wondered what he was doing there. He seemed out of place.

Years later, I wondered if Dad had put himself in the painting as the man just looking. Sometimes he would come into the room where I was doing my homework. I would hear him clearing his throat. I would turn to see him. Then he would leave. I wondered if he wanted to say something.

*

He says to T:

I will always remember my first exhibition opening at Peter Bray Gallery in 1956. After the hanging I walked through the rooms with the gallery director. The paintings looked more impressive with the lighting in the gallery than when balanced against the wall in the studio. However, I could not help comparing the work to Cézanne and Picasso, aware that it failed to live up to their accomplishments. Then I thought, 'This is not Paris 1910, this is Melbourne, Australia, 1956.' I had no doubt that I was making a serious comment, establishing an identity and a purpose for Australian art.

T: You could allow yourself to be impressed.

When Helen Ogilvie, the gallery director, pronounced her verdict, 'Simply marvellous,' I realised that the next time I would stand in this room, friends, relatives, artists and critics would be looking at what I had spent a year working on in the little shed in the backyard. They may not be thinking 'simply marvellous' or even 'a little bit marvellous'. I remember thinking, 'What if the critics failed to see what I was doing?'

On the tram going home after the hanging of the exhibition, I glanced at my fellow travellers sullenly reading their newspapers. I remember thinking how much easier to have a job in an office. Then, with no warning, Mother's words spoke from within me, 'Now look what you've done.' Although she had not been invited to the exhibition, I wanted her to see the paintings, to be proud of what I had done. I wanted her to see that I was a serious artist.

T: You wanted to return to that time when you had the power to make your mother smile, to make her proud of your accomplishments, to receive her applause.

Mother's 'now look what you've done' spoke to me as if the bottle of milk had slipped from my hands, not as the achievement of having an exhibition of paintings, my inaugural exhibition.

In *The Silent Woman*, Janet Malcolm writes, 'Art is theft, art is armed robbery, art is not pleasing your mother.' If this thought appealed to me, it would surely appeal to my father. I want to give him this quote but when speaking to T he says what comes into his head at that moment. I doubt that Janet Malcolm wrote this sentence just as it came into her head. A lot of thought went into crafting that sentence.

He says to T:

In my attempt to obliterate Mother's voice from within me, I came up with a private manifesto: Art is freeing oneself from one's mother's ambitions. Art is not seeking applause from one's mother...

T: . . .and art is not seeking the applause from whoever stands in the place of one's mother.

When Dad sold only one or two paintings at an exhibition, he would walk around the house gloomily muttering, 'I refuse to paint pretty pictures of flowers.'

*

In the next session he says:

I had grievances towards Mother. Helen's mother had grievances towards me for marrying her daughter. I remember the moment she seemed to accept me.

One Sunday morning about 4 am I was woken by Helen's tossing and churning accompanied by muffled cries of pain. She was seven months pregnant. I feared something was happening to the baby, but she would not let me ring the doctor, assuring me that she would be all right. I felt utterly helpless. In my ineptitude, I fetched a couple of aspros and a glass of water. The writhing and the muffled moaning continued for about an hour as I attempted to doze off to sleep. I did not know what to do when Helen became more and more flustered, kicking off the sheets and blankets as if the pain had possessed her. Then, after a silence, she let out a piercing scream. Something slithery had spilled from between her legs. It was bluish, streaked with blood and hardly bigger than my hand. I could barely recognise it for what it was. I remember thinking, 'This is not meant to be happening, this is not meant to be happening.'

I fumbled in Helen's handbag, searching for the doctor's phone number and then I heard a cry. The baby was alive.

The doctor arrived, cut the umbilical cord and wrapped the baby in a shawl. Despite the reassurance of his presence, my heart continued pounding. I got dressed. A taxi had been called to take Helen to the hospital. I was aware that something practical was demanded of me, so I scooped up the bloodstained sheets and got in the taxi with Helen and the baby, asking Helen helplessly what I should do with the bloodstained sheets.

When we arrived at the hospital, Helen was whisked away with the baby, leaving me in the taxi without her. It was nearly 8 am as I walked up the garden path of her mother's house. I knocked on the front door and as soon as it opened I thrust the bloodied sheets into Helen's mother's arms.

'Helen had her baby,' I said, handing the evidence. I was led into the dining room where she left me to take the sheets to the laundry. I helped myself to some cold toast and fumblingly spread it with strawberry jam as I tried to stop myself from bursting into tears. The enormity of what had happened was beginning to become clearer. Helen had given birth to her baby. When Helen's mother returned she referred to me as 'dear' and I knew then that I had been accepted.

That afternoon I went to the hospital to see Helen who was sitting up in bed. The baby was born two months premature and weighed only three pounds. The doctor told us that she was not likely to live. Two months later Helen went to the hospital and brought the baby home.

T: I'm astonished. It must have been traumatic for Helen and also for you.

I had never considered it traumatic. You have to realise that Helen is a stoic. The worst thing was my incompetence. I had no idea what to do. I felt utterly helpless. I knew nothing about childbirth. Fathers were not permitted at the birth.

T: What stopped you from ringing the doctor?

Helen didn't want me to interrupt the important man at 4 am on a Sunday morning.

T: And what about the two months when you didn't know if the baby would live?

I took Helen's expressed milk into the hospital on the way to work. One day I felt a wet patch on my legs and realised that the glass bottle was leaking. Fearing that the baby would die, I alighted at the next station and took a taxi to the hospital, leaving me with no money for my lunch. I explained to the nurse that the bottle was leaking, fearing that too much milk would be lost. It seemed that Helen had been expressing more milk than the baby could take in and the leftover milk was being fed to babies whose mothers did not have sufficient.

When I was eleven years old, Mum took me to visit a nurse who had worked at the hospital. As the nurse appeared from behind the flywire door of her home, Mum pointed at me and said, 'See, she didn't die.'

Eighteen months after my birth, Vicky was born; eighteen months later Freda was born, and then Charlotte. Four children in less than six years.

*

He tells T:

After the birth of our first and second child, I was very busy painting, determined to establish myself as an artist. I would have been happy to ignore Mother. The children had one grandmother; I didn't see why they needed another. Somehow Helen got it into her head that a grandmother should see her grandchildren. She was naïvely oblivious of Mother's hostility towards her, but as far as I was concerned, if she wanted to see Mother that was her business.

It did not surprise me when a rift opened up between them. Mother had given the children lollies and said, 'Don't tell Mummy.' Naturally the children did tell Mummy. 'She is teaching the children to tell lies,' Helen complained. 'She is teaching the children to keep secrets from their mother.' Mother would see the lollies as a way of endearing herself to her grandchildren. She would see it as her prerogative to spoil her grandchildren, but Helen expected me to tell Mother not to do this again. To appease her, I wrote a brief note as she had asked.

T: You wrote the note knowing it would antagonise your mother.

If this rupture between Helen and Mother had not happened then, sooner or later something else would have caused it.

Two weeks after Freda was born, Helen told me she intended visiting Mother with the new baby. I advised her not to go. That evening she reported on the visit.

'Mr Brack opened the door and said, "I'll get Mother" and when Mrs Brack came to the door, she shouted at me to go away, screaming at me.'

'Serves you right,' I said. 'I told you not to go.'

T: That must have been very distressing for Helen. Very distressing to be turned away with the new baby and then told 'serves you right'.

I told her not to go and she ignored my advice. What did she expect?

T: You were unsympathetic.

It justified severing my relationship with Mother. There was no announcement, no ceremonial cutting of a ribbon. Mother did not get in touch with me until ten years later when she rang to speak to me on the phone.

I wondered what would propel a grandmother to turn away her daughter-in-law holding a new baby, a two-year-old and a three-year-old by her side, having travelled on public transport to get there. The anger at her daughter-in-law must have been insurmountable.

I cannot remember Dad's mother giving me the lollies saying, 'Don't tell Mummy.' I can remember washing my hands in her bathroom basin. The soap was like a golden jewel, translucent brown. It wasn't opaque green like the soap we had at home.

Dad painted a picture called *Mother and Son*. He doesn't call it 'my mother' but given what I know about his relationship with his mother, it seems to me that it could be no one else.

He tells T:

After I had cut myself off from Mother, bouts of anger at her would remind me that she still had the power to upset me. I wanted to do something with this anger once and for all so I did the only thing I knew: I embarked on a painting called *Mother and Son*. Mother would not see it for the very reason that she had no interest in my paintings.

I remember painting the mother's face, pinched in, disapproving, ravenously scowling. The eyes squint through framed spectacles, staring into the distance. The son stands behind his mother, a helmet of thick hair carefully brushed, his collar neatly done up, his mouth turned up in the faintest hint of a smile. The son bursts with promise, refusing to be cowed by his mother's disapproval. One wonders how this shrivelled woman could have produced this statuesque young man glowing with the potential of all life ahead of him.

I had originally painted the mother and son against a drab grey-blue sky but then recalling Mother's comment that an artist merely 'dabbled', I found myself dabbling a pattern of white clouds, thinking, 'I will show you dabbling.' When I looked at it in reproduction several years later, I realised that the clouds were a caricature of clouds like a child would draw to fill in the background. They were thought balloons, empty with nothing to say. Nothing to say between the mother and the son.

T: The thought balloons say nothing but, as you describe it, the picture says a lot.

I regretted selling the painting. I had not expected it would sell. If it had not been sold, I would have burnt it. It was a shameful documentary of my thoughts about Mother, not that anyone would see it as 'my' mother. Mother did the best that she could. I don't blame her for wanting better things for her sons. I wanted better things for myself.

I am trying to remember my grandmother. Dad was trying to forget her. Severing a relationship with a parent does not cut them out of one's existence. The parent comes to us in dreams. The parent lives in our unconscious. The sculptor Henry Moore remembers rubbing his mother's back with liniment when he came home from school. She suffered terribly from rheumatism. Years later, in making the sculpture of a seated figure of a woman, he found himself 'unconsciously giving to its back the long-forgotten shape of the one I had so often rubbed as a boy.'

*

T: You wanted better things for yourself. Your mother wanted better things for you. What about your father?

There's an image of my father that has stayed with me from childhood. I had got up very early to go to the outside lavatory. On the way back I caught sight of my father wheeling his bike coming home from night shift. 'So this is what work is,' I thought. It explained Mother's eagerness that we not have a job like our father. It wasn't just the expression on my father's face, it is what happened after. When he saw me, his face transformed, and I knew then that he concealed his dejection from me.

If I was disheartened by the work in the insurance office, shift work in the brewery would be even more disheartening. Office work was 9 am to 5 pm. I was sitting at a desk adding up figures. After mastering what was required of me an onerous, dreary boredom set in. I should have felt ecstatic leaving work at the end of the day, but boredom had destroyed any capacity for rejoicing. I remember walking along the street thinking that I should not be feeling like this in a job so much 'better' than my father's. If it were not for the Hill of Content bookshop and enrolling in the night class at the gallery school, I do not know what would have become of me.

After returning from the army I found myself once again in the city at 5 pm, waiting for Stephens in the doorway of his office in Collins

Street. We were having a drink after work. As I waited, I was struck by the uniformly grim expressions on the faces of the office workers walking to the railway station. Despite leaving work to make their way home, the dejection of the work had fixed itself on their faces. The thought came to me, 'I could put this into a painting.'

These people who worked in offices in the day retreated to the suburbs in the night. They appeared to be haunted by existential angst, an unidentified ennui which was more than the boredom of the job. I stood in the doorway sketching the figures walking down the street, striving to capture their facial expressions, their clothes, their mannerisms. I had planned on painting an anonymous crowd in the distance, but given that the impersonal crowd is a cliché, close up there would have to be individual portraits, otherwise the painting would fail through facile overstatement. It struck me as almost eerie to be sketching within three feet of so many people, none of whom took the slightest notice of me. Although the faces in my painting were based on actual people, I altered them to represent generic types, painting the recognisable face of John Stephens and Helen's father who worked in Collins Street.

All portraits are, at some level, a reflection of the artist. I was aware that in painting the figures walking down the street I was investing each with the same lack of enchantment that I had experienced working in the office.

T: You are telling me that *Collins St 5pm* had its genesis in your memory of walking down the street in your first job working in an office. Perhaps it has its genesis further back in the memory of your father returning home from shift work. If that is so, the person who had 'inspired' the painting was of necessity absent from it. Your father was not walking home from work at 5 pm carrying a briefcase wearing a jacket and a tie. He was coming home in the early hours of the morning, his clothes tainted with the smell of the factory where he worked.

I want my father to make some reference to his father. I want to believe that his father's work had some bearing on his own.

He continues with what he has previously said in interview:

It was arrogant of me to see the workers like this. The painting appeared to be saying, 'Look at those pathetic little people with their boredom and their dull lives. I am different from them. I am an artist.' At the art school we considered ourselves superior to the office worker, the factory worker, the tradesman. We might be poor, but we had a vocation, we were not working for a boss. I should have known that the lives of the office workers were as complex as mine, if not more. In the arrogance of youth, I had no respect for the lives of my parents. I just wanted to get away from them. I wanted to get away from the poverty and dismalness of my childhood.

Through no fault of my own *Collins St 5pm* became a famous Australian painting. You would think that an artist would be pleased that his work had become so well known, but it means that one is permanently identified with that work. The irony is that the work that creates a sense of identity and belonging was painted by a man who felt that he never belonged.

T: Perhaps none of us feel we belong. Perhaps that is our belonging.

*

In 1953, two years before Dad painted *Collins Street 5pm*, he painted *The New House*, a painting of a man and a woman standing together in a living room. The man has one hand in the pocket of his suit jacket, the other around the woman's waist, clasping her like a doll. One of the woman's hands rests lightly near his tie while her head nestles on his shoulder. The man is in profile, sternly cold. The woman looks directly at us, smiling. The man is wearing a suit, the woman wears a dress, a frilled apron around her waist. The painting appears to be saying,

'Look at these people proudly standing in their new house. They think the new house will make them happy. I know better.'

I wondered about the house in which Dad was raised.

He says to T:

I remember one of the last times I saw Mother. I had visited her to collect my birth certificate. I was annoyed with her frustration fossicking in the kitchen cupboard drawer, so I removed myself to the front room, a room reserved for visitors which I was now qualified to enter. In Mother's absence my eyes did a circuit of the room, noticing the couch, the chairs, the wireless, the little figurines imprisoned in a glass cabinet. There was not a single book and not a single picture on the wall and although the room was cleaned and dusted as a showcase for visitors, to my knowledge few visitors ever came.

Mother found the birth certificate, which she thrust into my hands—as if in handing over the record of my birth she was relinquishing the son whose birth it recorded. Later, when I looked at the two signatures under my name, I wondered how it was that I had been born from these two people who were so different from me in every way imaginable.

T: They may have been wondering the same thing themselves.

I imagined I had successfully extricated myself from Mother and from Pater. They had occasionally come to me in dreams. Never before since talking to you have they returned night after night. *You* have made them return. You have surreptitiously laid out the red carpet for them.

T: Our parents live on in our unconscious. It is what we are working on here. It is the material we work with.

My unconscious takes me to Kafka's letter to his father.

'Dearest Father, You asked me recently why I maintain that I am afraid of you. As usual, I was unable to think of any answer to your question, partly for the very reason that I am afraid of you…'

Kafka never sent the forty-seven-page letter to his father, and since the executor of his will did not burn all his writings as instructed, the letter Kafka's father never read can now be read by anyone who searches on the internet.

Kafka wrote, 'A book can be the axe for the frozen sea within us. There is no point in a book that does not wake us up, disturb us.'

I give these words to my father.

He tells T:

The artist works with the unconscious. The painting is wide open to interpretation, its meaning is inexhaustible. A painting can be the axe for the frozen sea within us. There is no point in a painting that does not wake us up, disturb us.

T: Are you telling me that there is no point to being here if it does not wake you up, disturb you? Are you telling me that you are prepared to be disturbed, to break the frozen sea inside you?

I refused to paint pretty pictures of flowers.

*

In the next session he says to T:

I see you have a vase of poppies in your room. In my painting *The Bar*, I put a vase of poppies on the bar.

The Bar was inspired by one of the great paintings of the nineteenth century, Manet's *A Bar at the Folies-Bergère*. I was struck by the observation that the life it reflects so vividly and sensuously no longer exists. It seemed like a good idea, almost a century later, to do another painting of the bar, a painting of a life that does exist.

I painted it in 1954 when pubs closed at 6 pm. Now *that* life no longer exists. In Manet's painting, a barmaid stands in front of a mirror reflecting the other side of the bar. My barmaid also stands in front of a mirror. The bar in my painting is a synthesis of several bars, and although the barmaid is a portrait, she was actually an attendant in a milkbar, a woman who seemed to fit better with my conception of a barmaid. Years later, I realised that in her regal domination of the small space, her hand firmly on the cloth, the barmaid bears an uncanny resemblance to Helen.

Someone once asked the poet Les Murray if he was a tall poppy. 'No, I am a gorgeous spreading hydrangea,' he said.

He says to T:

Most bars have no flowers at all. The vase of Iceland poppies symbolised the suburbia of the 1950s. These were the sort of bought flowers people had in vases. Someone once asked if I was a tall poppy. 'No,' I said, 'I am the host of golden daffodils I saw wandering lonely as a child.'

*

I read somewhere that, 'John Brack sees the twentieth century in a state of precarious balance.'

In the next session, he says to T:

Every so often I return to that moment when I literally fell into the gutter. I remember thinking, 'This is the still point of the turning world.' The actual fall was a blessed relief from the increasing dread that I would succumb to dementia. I lived in terror that I would end up like my friend Perceval who needed a minder and could no longer paint as he once did. All my life I have lived with a sense of ominousness as if things were in a state of precarious balance, things about to fall.

I was born in 1920, two years after the end of the First World War. I was nineteen at the beginning of the Second World War. In that formative time of my life between the wars it is understandable that a 'sensitive' child would pick up a premonition of uncertainty from the headlines in the newspaper, the news on the radio, talk about an impending war after the war that was meant to end all wars. I often feared that a tower of blocks would topple over within me. I feared that I would fall into the abyss of oblivion. Painting did something with this sense of things about to fall. The act of painting was like stamping one's foot on a piece of paper to stop it from flying away in the wind. The control over the paintbrush gave me the illusion of holding things still, of holding myself from falling.

This sense of precariousness drew me to find the subject of my paintings in the form of jockeys, gymnasts and ballroom dancers poised in precarious balance almost to the point of slipping or falling over. Everyday items were positioned in a state of falling—knives and forks, pens and pencils. Floorboards and Persian carpets were placed at disconcerting angles, suggestive of falling. I knew that if it were not for painting, I myself would feel as if I was toppling into the abyss.

My father's sense of things about to fall may have been exacerbated by what I saw as the self-medication to relieve it. I remember ironing my school dress in the kitchen when Dad would come in wearing his dressing gown. He would say nothing. He would pour himself a glass of water, drop the Alka-Seltzer tablet into the water, watch it fizz up, and as I moved the iron back and forth over the blue, yellow and white checks, I would glance at the fizzing water, aware of Dad waiting for the tablet to be completely dissolved and then gulping. I knew the Alka-Seltzer was for the hangover from the previous night's drinking which was an attempt to take the edge off the depression.

Depression inhabits the house. It asks to be respected. One fears that if it is not respected, it will do more than fizz up and dissolve; it will obliterate the bearer of it and consequently the whole family. I often sensed that at any moment someone could pull an imaginary tablecloth off our kitchen table and everything on the surface would fall—plates, knives, forks and spoons. It was not only the twentieth century that was in a state of precarious balance. It was our own three-bedroom weatherboard home in the suburb of Surrey Hills.

He says to T:

Sometimes in the morning the precariousness would strike in that moment between waking up and starting on the day. Drinking alleviated the sense of things about to fall. Fortunately, my muscle memory kept me painting, and I never failed to come up with ideas for painting, even if they were variations on a theme. Ultimately, I maintained the discipline required of an artist helped along by the ordered, predictable routine of family life. Once or twice the break in routine when Helen was in hospital sent me into a state of anxiety, added to the fact that I was required to do something about the dinner and the household chores.

Thankfully these visits to you are the same time every day. I am framed within the fifty-minute session.

*

When you live with a painting, you come to see things in it you didn't see at first sighting. If the artist is your father you cannot see the painting separately from your experience of him as a father.

Dad's painting *The Scissors Shop* hung in the house I lived in when I left home. Three rows of surgical scissors are opened and shut in shades of black, dark aqua, blue-green. They are placed on three shelves against a lurid pink background suggestive of opened flesh. On the top of the cabinet two hands are spread out, palms facing downward onto the glass. The hands are those of Dad's friend Hal Hattam, a gynaecologist who collected paintings. Once, when he was giving Dad a lift in his car, the glove box sprung open and his surgical scissors tumbled out.

I lived with the painting *The Scissors Shop*. I saw it subliminally. Sometimes I stood and looked at it without distraction. Sometimes I pictured the hands on the top of the cabinet picking up the scissors and cutting into open flesh.

Dad didn't just *draw* pictures of knives and scissors, he used them. I remember looking through his bookshelves, taking out Céline's *Death on The Instalment Plan*. I opened it up. A Stanley knife had been used to cut a small rectangle from within the pages of the book. Inside the cavern made by the cutting lay a bank book in Dad's name.

The menace was in the threat. The premonition that things would fall. Dad walked up and down the hallway clenching his fists. He restrained his anger in the house, but his silence radiated aggression. Once, as Mum and I cleared up after lunch, he returned after leaving for the studio, said something provocative and then left before we could reply.

'He needs to do that,' Mum said. 'He needs to stir up some anger before he gets back to painting.'

*

Dad died in February 1999. A few years after his death, a retrospective exhibition of his work was held at the National Gallery of Victoria. Almost all his paintings were displayed in the exhibition. He was 'speaking' to us in his paintings. He was also speaking to us in grey font printed directly onto the wall: 'What I paint most is what interests me most, that is, people; the human condition.'

A pang of anger hit me as I read those words. I wanted to say, 'You might have painted pictures of your four daughters but what would you know of the human condition of any one of us?'

Competing voices arose from within me.

'How lucky you are to have those pictures of you.'

'That *Collins Street 5pm* is a masterpiece.'

'But what help was he when I fell off my bike and Mum wasn't home?'

'What did he say when I was eight and didn't know who fought who in the Second World War? "You dill."'

'Look at how marvellous the paintings of the pencils and pens, how imaginative, how ingenious.'

'Where were you when we were on holiday at the beach?'

'We are so lucky to have those etchings of the four of us.'

'Remember the gloom when paintings didn't sell...'

'But look at the brilliance of those portraits and the nudes on the Persian rugs.'

'And where were you when one of us was ill?'

'Those pictures of the postcards are superb: the colours, the craftsmanship...'

'Where was your support for Mum?'

'But look at those portraits of Mum when she was younger; she looks severe in the later portrait, but also regal and self-possessed.'

'How lucky to see the inner life of your father in the paintings, the lifetime's work. It's a mighty achievement.'

'What I paint most is what interests me most, that is, people; the human condition.'

You rarely showed much 'interest' in us. We are people. We are human.

I wanted to say to my father, 'It's not just that you didn't show much interest in us; it is the grandiosity of "the human condition". What gives you the entitlement to speak on behalf of others, the omnipotence to know something about all humans from your own limited experience?' The audacity of it. Mum would never claim to speak of the human condition.

An uneasiness arose as I became alert to other writers and artists referring to 'the human condition'. In reconsidering my resistance to it, I remembered listening to Mum's recording of the American comedian Ruth Draper. As a society hostess she gives a monologue translating Dante for her Italian lesson. She concludes with her translation:

'Midway in the journey of my life
I found myself in a dark forest
because the direct way was lost.'

How could one 'find oneself' in the dark forest? I wondered. If you were sensible, wouldn't you see yourself going into the forest? And if you saw yourself going in, wouldn't you find your way out?

Yet I knew from my own adolescence that I had not *decided* to ask the questions, 'Who am I? Where do I belong? What is my purpose in life?' The questions had arisen from within. I had *found myself* asking those questions midway between childhood and adulthood.

Isn't this 'the human condition'? We *find* ourselves lost in the dark forest, not having known how we arrived there, seeking to find a way out?

Now I understood it. My own idiosyncratic wonderings were not particular to me but an aspect of being human. If we keep our thoughts and feelings private, we have no way of knowing that others share the same troubles and worries that we do.

*

He tells T:

I remember when I knew that I was not alone in the world, not a freakish isolate, that my anguish was an aspect of being human. I was fifteen when I read a short story. Two adolescent boys meet on the beach where their families are staying for the summer holidays. As they swim, dabble in rock pools and laze in the sun, they talk about their worries about what they are going to be when they grow up. Each of the boys does not want to be what their father wants them to be and yet, in choosing what they want to do, they fear their father's disappointment. One of the boys does not want to enter the family business. He wants to be an actor. The other wants to write. At the end of the holidays, they return to their homes in different towns, each feeling the loss of the friendship they have made over the summer holiday.

My parents could not afford a summer holiday at the beach. I did not have a friend, but I knew then that other boys had the same questions as I did, questions that I had never articulated to myself. This is what adolescence is, I thought, this worry about finding what one wants to do in life, not what one's parents want for us. This is universal.

T: As an adolescent you were reassured at not being alone.

And then as an adult I read André Malraux's novel *La Condition Humaine* and Hannah Arendt's philosophical treatise *The Human Condition*. Magritte named a painting *La Condition Humaine*. The titles impressed me. Through our understanding of the human condition we connect through literature and art. This was my thinking when an interviewer asked, 'How do you choose what to paint?' I found myself responding: 'What I paint most is what interests me most, that is, people; the human condition. The artist's motive is to understand and to illuminate for others.'

When the interview was written up in the newspaper, my reference to 'the human condition' was used as a headline for the interview.

Helen would not let it go. 'The arrogance of it. I mean, I ask you! Who do you think you are? The human condition.'

T: Perhaps that is what we are doing here, exploring 'the human condition'.

*

When tidying up for visitors, we could never find a place for a single snakeskin shoe with a silver buckle. The leather lining was embossed with the name of a shop in London, written in gold cursive script. Without any designated purpose, it sat on a mantelpiece, a bookshelf, a toy box: an emblem of my mother's childhood.

There was not a single remnant from my father's childhood, no photograph, nothing.

He says to T:

You want me to say whatever comes into my mind. Nothing comes to mind. Nothing. My mind has gone blank. I once painted a portrait of Kim Bonython who was known as an art collector, racing car identity, jazz enthusiast, bon vivant. After the portrait was completed, I received a letter from him asking if in 'that blank area in the top right-hand corner of the picture' I could paint his celebrated chequered cap. I wrote back saying, 'There is no blank area in the top right-hand corner of the picture' but that if he liked I would paint a separate painting of his treasured cap. As an art collector you would think that he would know that the blank in the painting is saying something.

T: The blank in the painting is saying something as the silence in this room is saying something.

The blank in the painting is nothing like the blank of the canvas before one starts a painting. Every time one faces the blank canvas one is struck with terror. You would think it would diminish over the years, but it never does. To alleviate the terror, I always started a new picture before finishing the last.

T: What was your first experience of terror?

I was ten years old. Mother was one of nine children. We were visiting one of her sisters who lived in the country. I had never been to the country before. After lunch Mother and Aunty Ivy did the washing up while the rest of us set out on a little path weaving its way through the gum trees. Lindsay and I took up the rear walking in silence, deep in our own thoughts. The only sounds were the twittering of birds and the occasional twig snapping underfoot. I stopped to take a stone out of my shoe and then continued on the path, while Lindsay walked ahead. The thought came to me, 'I am all alone in this world.' The silence was broken by the piercing cry of a bird soaring overhead, a shrill cry echoing through the landscape as if the cry was calling from inside me. I was hit with the terror of the question, 'Who am I? What am I doing in this world?' The question struck me like the piercing of an arrow.

The echo of the cry persisted until I came upon the others peering into an empty well. My father picked up a stone and dropped it into the well. A few seconds later the echo announced that it had reached its destination. A dread came into my stomach as if I myself had been dropped into the well. I picked up a stone and dropped it in and then picked up another and another. I was aware of Lindsay speaking to me, but I felt cut off from him and everybody else.

When we arrived home, my father paused before going in the front door, remarking to all of us and no one in particular, 'It's nice to have the concrete under the feet.'

Later that night I recalled the terror. I assumed it was particular to me but then I wondered if my father had also experienced the terror, knowing that it was not something one could speak about to another, least of all one's father.

T: You wondered about having a rapport with your own father as you had with Helen's father.

In 1947, at the age of twenty-seven, I painted a picture of a boy running, his eyes bulging in terror, his mouth wide open in a silent scream. I called it *Little Boy Lost*, an expression of that romantic feeling characteristic of young people, saying, 'I am unhappy, lost to myself.' Now I see it as self-indulgent and naïve.

T: Your cynicism protects you.

Nothing protected me from the terror. Every so often an injection of terror reinserted itself, accompanied by the anxiety of the thought, 'Who am I? What should I be doing with my life?' The discovery that I wanted to be an artist initially relieved me of the terror, but it returned when I was not painting and invariably resurfaced when faced with the blank canvas.

T: Do you feel the terror now?

No, I don't. I am at the still point of the turning world.

*

When I was fifteen, Mum took me to see Barry Humphries performing in his one-man show as Mrs Everage. As Mum says, 'In those days nobody had seen a man dressed up as a woman. That is what made it terribly funny.' Over the years Mrs Everage became more outspoken, more daring, playing to larger audiences in mainstream theatres, not the little hall where I had first seen her. Elevated to 'Dame Edna', she wore a wig, ornate spectacles and garishly beaded costumes, not the hat, simple frock and handbag of the housewife from Moonee Ponds.

I do not know Dad's thoughts on Mrs Everage, but I do know what he said in interview about painting a portrait of her.

He tells T:

When I first saw Barry Humphries as Mrs Everage, I recognised myself—another man feeling antipathy towards his mother. Barry took up dressing as the suburban housewife that his mother was, satirically mocking her in public on stage, flaunting his disregard for his mother. Compared to Barry's mother, Mother had nothing to complain about.

When Mrs Everage had become a cultural icon, I was asked to paint a portrait of Barry Humphries in the role of Mrs Everage.

The struggle with the painting felt insurmountable. I had never painted a portrait of one person posing as another. When I muttered,

'This is terrible, this is disastrous,' Barry kindly suggested giving up but I assured him that my mutterings were my highest form of praise. It wasn't just that it was the portrait of one person posing as another. As the sittings progressed, my rapport with Barry fuelled my disdain for my own mother. Barry's mocking of his mother gave me permission to unleash on my own and I found myself having to resist the combined force of what we recognised in each other. We were like two boys egging each other on, pulling the wings off flies.

As Barry stepped out of the dress he wore as Mrs Everage, the thought came to me: 'One cannot easily step out of the influence of one's mother.' Here was Barry, more obviously than me, getting back at his mother, making an art form of it. The grotesqueness of it both attracted and repulsed me.

When I looked at the finished painting and saw Mrs Everage looking at me from the canvas—her large, gloved hands splayed over the couch, her eyes leering at me—I realised I was looking at a vulture.

T: A vulture.

It was not only our mothers that Barry and I had in common. We both took solace for what troubled us in drink. When Barry arrived in my studio at 10 am for the sitting, he brought with him not only the costume, the wig, the powder and the lipstick, but a bottle of that ghastly tasting Italian drink, Fernet Branca.

'What's wrong with beer or wine?' I asked him.

'This is thirty-five percent alcohol,' he said.

I refused his offer of a swig, saying, 'It would be an offence to Mrs Everage to be drinking on the job.'

A year or so after finishing the portrait, I heard that Barry was found bashed lying in a carpark outside a pub after a heavy bout of drinking. He was taken to a private hospital to dry out. It rattled me when I heard the news, not only for Barry's sake but for my own. I told myself that it would not happen to me, as I was not drinking thirty-five percent alcohol at ten o'clock in the morning. Instead of taking what happened to Barry as a warning, I ignored it. When I was found in the gutter drunk and sent to hospital to dry out, I had to confront not only the humiliation, but my own hubris.

T: *And now you are here.*

And now I am here. Were it not for falling in the gutter, I would have lost my mind. I remember the fear when the paintbrush first slipped from my hand. I knew it was a sign of something ominous.

T: What did you do with that fear?

I poured myself a drink.

*

The next session he says to T:

The memory of the paintbrush falling from my hand takes me to the first night home from the army when something bigger than a paintbrush fell from me—the hope that Mother would approve of my decision to be an artist.

A few years later I remember looking at a reproduction of Rembrandt's *The Return of the Prodigal Son*. The Bible parable tells us that the prodigal son returns, asking for forgiveness for having squandered his inheritance. I had done nothing to warrant my parents' forgiveness. I was anything but prodigal. I was the eldest son who had to leave school to contribute to the finances of the family because my father was too poor to keep me at school. I had brought money into the family, not squandered it. I was the son who had ensured that his younger brother stayed at school, not that I begrudged Lindsay this opportunity. After studying Rembrandt's painting *The Return of the Prodigal Son* I embarked on a version of my own.

The Bible parable makes no reference to the mother. My painting gives prominence to the mother. I remember painting the smirk on her face. I remember taking a ruler to flatten her chest as if she had never nursed a child. In my painting the father sits blankly, resigned. The son sits between his mother and his father, looking at his plate downcast, dispirited. The son appears to be going through the motions of eating his meal as if obediently doing what he is told. The son's hand is poised on the knife in the act of eating his dinner. The mother's hand is forcefully grasping a knife but with no dinner in front of her, there is no apparent purpose to the knife. The brother hovers in the doorway.

T: The painting is a message, a private declaration of your experience of returning home after your time in the army.

It is a message to myself. My parents would never see the painting, not having sufficient interest to come to the exhibition where it was shown. Stephens bought the painting. He knew the meaning of it. I had no reason to give the painting any further thought until I was asked to look at the quality of the reproduction for a book. This time I saw what I had not seen when focused on solving the problem of the painting. I saw the father, corpse-like, grim, scowling. I saw the disheartened son obediently poised over his frugal dinner. I saw the mother in her butcher's apron, clenching a knife in her fist, a smirk on her face. Then I saw what I had not seen before. I saw the prospect of the mother's hand rising and striking down the knife in a gesture of castration.

T: You saw what you feared of your mother.

*

In the next session he says:

Early in our marriage, Helen was sitting on the couch reading *The Brothers Karamazov*, turning the pages and chuckling to herself. 'It's not a comic book,' I said. She was only laughing, she said, 'because now I know where you get your ideas from.'

Helen had accused me of getting my ideas from Dostoevsky but where did she get her ideas? She got them from me, of course. She was only reading *The Brothers Karamazov* because I had suggested that she did. You have to remember that she was barely twenty-one when we first met. I was twenty-seven. In the beginning she got her ideas from me but over the years it seemed that she got more and more ideas of her own.

We had gone to dinner at Mac and Jessie's house. Gordon and Kate were also present. After dinner the women went into the kitchen while Mac, Gordon and I adjourned to the sitting room where we discussed the problem of romanticism in poetry. When Mac left to fetch another bottle of wine, the thought came to me: none of our fathers would have engaged in a conversation about literature. We were ambitious, clever boys from the working class who had received a grant to have an education. We had come far from our working-class beginnings.

When Mac returned, he reported that the women had finished the washing up and suggested that we invite them to come in and listen in to our conversation. As the wives sat down where Mac indicated they were to sit, I began to have doubts about the wisdom of this invitation. We continued our discussion where we had left off, but the ambiance had changed and I was aware that we were performing for an audience. Not only that, Helen and Kate found a way of inserting themselves into the discussion, offering their own ill-formed opinions.

We had barely driven off in the taxi when Helen remarked on how 'ridiculous' we looked. She accused me of 'pomposity', of 'showing off', of 'competing' with Gordon and Mac. Instead of listening in and learning something from us as Mac had envisaged, Helen had launched into ridicule. 'We were *allowed* to listen in to your conversation,' she said.

Helen was right. We *were* competing and showing off, but it was the way that she said it. She said it with contempt. I should have trusted my instinct. I knew that it was a mistake to invite the women in. Mac wanted to impress them. We were impressed with ourselves. We had sought each other out. Our wives were middle class. They were not thinking, 'Look how far we've come.'

T: You saw yourselves as 'lower' because of your class. You saw the women as 'lower' because they were women, despite the fact that they were middle class.

In the next session he says to T:

Helen had been brought up in the genteel upper class where she learnt to talk to people, introduce people, shake hands. I had been brought up in a house of very few visitors with few social outings. Helen had insisted I come to her parents' house for Christmas but it was Rudy who insisted I make the aeroplane flight to Sydney to meet collectors who were considering buying a painting. I loathed these events which took a whole day away from painting.

From the moment we arrived, I found myself counting the minutes until it was time to go home. In my resentment at having to be there I would hear Helen's declaration: 'I have never tasted anything so delicious in my whole life.' I then recalled her hovering over the kitchen table, dipping her spoon into the saucepan, scraping the remains as her dinner. I would observe her nodding at the man next to her, laughing, occasionally saying a few words and then on the plane going home she would tell me, 'such an odious little man' and accuse me of sitting there glumly looking at my watch.

T: You are telling me how much work Helen put into your career.

That was the agreement. Yvonne looked after Arthur, Mary looked after Perceval and Lynn did a superb job looking after Freddy.

T: The artists had their wives. Helen was an artist. Who was her wife?

She seemed to manage perfectly well without one.

After the lunch Mum would receive a bottle of French perfume or a bunch of roses couriered as a gift from Rudy. He would know that Dad would not have come to the lunch if it were not for Mum's insistence.

In the next session he says to T:

Helen was equally at ease in the social gatherings of her parents' social circle as she was at the art openings, the artist dinner parties. I remember when we went to Sydney for the opening of an exhibition. For the first time in my life nearly all the paintings were sold. The triumph unnerved me. If so many paintings were sold, I told myself, they must be too accessible. Whatever the reason, there was something wrong.

The night after the opening, I had expected a quiet evening at the home of the artist friend where we were staying but it seemed that a dinner party had been arranged in my honour. There was no escape. I loathed these gatherings. I refused to demean myself by indulging in the performance expected of an artist.

As the evening progressed, the bonhomie, the competitiveness and the congratulations left me feeling more and more morose until the pantomime became intolerable. A woman grabbed me by the hand and pulled me up from my chair announcing, 'Let's dance.'

'Let him go, Yvette,' someone said as if I was a puppet. As the guest of honour, it would have been churlish to slink off hoping no one would notice. Helen would be furious. But then, feeling more and more ill at ease, I got up, opened the door and went outside, beyond caring if anyone noticed my departure.

I found myself walking up the hill away from the house until I reached a path leading to a cliff-top. I stood there gazing down into the waves swirling below me. The pull of the waves was more than the feeling of gravity. I glanced down every few seconds, looked away and resumed looking at the waves. I saw myself as if outside looking in. I was observing myself standing on the cliff-top looking down.

Nature was not my preferred location for a suicide. In moments of angst and terror which might have prompted such a deed, I made sure there was always a painting to work on.

It seemed that I was not the only person observing. As I stood staring at the waves, I heard a man speaking to me. 'Hello there. It's all right, it's all right.' I looked up. 'Come with me,' he said, approaching and taking me by the arm. Something in his demeanour put me under a spell. I lost my autonomy. I did as he asked. I allowed him to take me by the arm and steer me down the hill away from the cliff-top. I normally shirk at other people's touch but this time I found myself meekly surrendering.

We arrived at the front door of an unpretentious house where he took out his keys, opened the door and directed me down the hallway and into the kitchen where he put the kettle on the stove.

The house felt reminiscent of the house I grew up in. The sparse tidiness reassured me. The light from a single globe hanging from the ceiling was more comforting to me than the dim light and the cultivated bohemian disorder of the house I had fled. My host inquired if I had children as he poured a cup of tea from a teapot dressed in a knitted tea cosy which I had not seen since childhood. A woman entered the room, tying the belt on her dressing gown as she sat down to join us. 'This is Marjorie,' the man told me.

Marjorie told me that they had recently become grandparents. I told her about the birth of our first child and then found myself laughing at a joke I made, pleased that my host and hostess also found it amusing, accepting my offer of a little gift of humour. It was not until after midnight when my host walked me to the place where I was staying. We shook hands. I never saw him again.

T: What drew you to this man?

He reminded me of my father. He and Marjorie were the antithesis of the artists at the dinner party. They were ordinary people like my parents, but unlike my parents they had no expectations of me. The sound of the man's voice saying, 'It's all right, it's all right' convinced me that at that moment it would be all right.

Neither Mother nor my father had ever come to one of my exhibitions as far as I knew. It would not matter that they didn't understand the paintings, it would have been enough that they had come.

T: You didn't want the congratulations. You wanted your parents to see the exhibition, to accept you as an artist. You put your trust in this fellow who guided you away from the cliff-top. You are putting your trust in me. Like the man on the cliff-top, I am reassuring you that it will be all right.

*

In the next session he says:

I trusted my instincts following the man down the cliff-top. It would have served me better if I had trusted my instincts on other occasions—like the time I was bullied into doing a portrait.

The trustees at a university wanted a double portrait of the first chancellor and vice chancellor of the university. I said I wouldn't do it. I did not welcome the challenge of doing a double portrait, which I had never done before. I suggested that a photograph by a professional photographer would be considerably cheaper but they wanted a painting and apparently there was no other artist of my stature who could do it.

One of the men was Sir Garfield Barwick, whose advice two years before to the governor-general led to the dismissal of the Whitlam Labor government. On doing my homework before the first sitting, I learnt that Barwick's family was so impoverished he often walked miles to school without shoes on. He had gone to a selective-entry high school then to university followed by a brilliant career as a barrister before becoming chief justice of the High Court. We had both come from poor families and risen to the height of our professions but, in a manner I can't quite identify, Barwick let it be known that he was superior to a man whose job was putting paint on canvas.

After seeing a photo of the double portrait, I asked Mum about having Garfield Barwick for lunch as, usually, the sitters were invited after the morning sitting. I wondered what a man who looked as solemn and austere as Barwick would make of the décor of the kitchen and the meal Mum provided. Shopping lists, bills and gallery invitations were propped up between the salt and pepper shakers on the kitchen table which would have been wiped down with a sponge. The plates were scratched floral Royal Doulton, the knives and forks well used. Mum wasn't prepared to give up her morning painting time preparing lunch so she usually flung some sausages on the stove and then nipped out and picked some lettuce and rocket from the garden to make a salad. Dad provided cheese he had bought on his Monday day off.

He tells T:

In that awkward moment after the sitting, I invited Barwick to lunch. The offer was declined. The man who had walked several miles to school, often without shoes on, had a driver waiting for him to transport him to his next destination. It did not surprise me. Naturally, my observations of Barwick entered the portrait. On seeing the finished work Barwick reportedly said that as a work of art he didn't have to like it. The verdict of his wife was said to be 'unprintable'. The trustees may have assumed that given my eminence as an artist and the eminence of the two men, the portrait would depict the grandiose splendour befitting a portrait of the first chancellor and vice chancellor of the university. Serves them right. I told them I didn't want to do it. I should have trusted my instincts and refused.

There's an irony to it. I had suggested a photograph instead of a painting. A photograph of me standing with the two men sitting in front of the portrait was put into the National Portrait Gallery.

More people would see the photograph of the portrait than the original in the basement of a university where it may have been demoted given its reception.

T: You saw in Garfield Barwick a man who had betrayed his origins in sacking a Labor prime minister.

I know now that we cannot escape our origins. The past never leaves us. I had thought that in not having contact with my parents I would be free of them. They wanted their sons to be successful. Suddenly, at age sixty, I didn't feel the elation one might expect of a successful man. Success made me feel like an impostor. I wanted to hide in the studio away from the clamour demanding the next picture. When prices rose beyond what I had ever imagined, I knew there was something wrong. You'd think I would be joyously happy not having to worry about money, but I wasn't.

T: How do you explain it?

It's an atavistic sense of guilt. It is a sin I would have to atone for. It is guilt that I was so much more financially successful than my father. It was my fault for allowing it to happen.

T: You felt guilt at being more financially successful than your father. What about your mother?

I would have thought that Mother would have enjoyed my success, as she had when I did so well at school. I remember sitting alone when one of the children passed on the message that Mother wanted me to ring her. I had not heard from Mother for fifteen years. The unexpected reference to Mother sent a nervous tremor through me. What could she want?

After dinner I looked up the telephone book, dialled the number and listened apprehensively to the phone ringing. She had discovered that there was going to be a television program about me. You would think this would be a mark of my success, a half-hour television program about my work. She wanted to know if I was going to say something bad about her.

T: You wanted something more.

I should have known better. Serves me right.

In the next session he says to T:

Every January Helen took the children to the beach while I stayed at home painting. It's not as if I missed them, but their absence put me in a limbo, waiting for their return.

One morning I had settled into painting when I remembered that I had left some tubes of paint inside the house. I opened the back door and stepped into the silence which was instantly broken by the ringing of the phone. Helen always answered the phone and since she wasn't there, it continued to ring as if daring me to pick it up. When I closed the back door to return to the studio, disconcertingly, it stopped. An uneasiness gripped me for the rest of the day, and in the evening as I walked down the path to collect the letters from the letterbox, the thought came to me, 'What if it was Mother? What if Mother was ringing, knowing Helen was away? What if she wanted to say something to me?'

T: As long as a parent is still living, we never give up hope of reconciliation. The same is true of the parent wishing to be reconciled with the child.

I remember the return from the holiday at the beach. The journey back home brought the increasing sense of loss that the holiday was over. I remember one year coming into the kitchen and seeing Dad standing alone. There were fewer plates in the drying rack and the room seemed tidier than usual. 'Oh, so you're back,' he said, more as an observation than a welcome home. None of us ran up to him like children do in films saying, 'Daddy, we missed you.'

The holiday was not just the pleasure of the beach. It was a holiday from Dad. Mum was free of her anxiety about pleasing him, of having to get back in a hurry to get his lunch. Even the sound of his voice,

'Oh, so you're back,' summoned up the apprehension that if something was wrong it must be 'my' or 'our' fault.

*

He tells T:

Every year before the summer holiday I fell into a deep despondency on the anticipation of Christmas dinner at Helen's family home. I will never understand why Helen insisted I come. It's not as if I was a source of entertainment.

One year, three days before Christmas, I left to stay at Lindsay's house. The next year I booked myself into the Southern Cross Hotel. As I entered the lobby, a sparkling Christmas tree exacerbated my misery and the sight of two young women wearing reindeer hats made me want to shake some sense into them, saying, 'There is nothing to laugh about, you fatheads.'

I remember sitting in the hotel room looking at the textured wallpaper, the garishly patterned bedspread, the ghastly print hanging on the wall. I imagined the room erupting in laughter, mocking me for having chosen to come here. I opened the fridge to get some ice for the whiskey I had bought but the miniature bottles of spirits shook my sense of reality as if I had fallen down the rabbit hole. I might have escaped Helen and the prospect of Christmas dinner at her parents' house but I was now held prisoner, although I could not say who it was who had imprisoned me or what crime I had committed.

The next day I returned home and accompanied Helen and the children to Christmas dinner.

T: You have told me it is abject for a parent to ask a child for money. You have told me of your atavistic guilt for earning significantly more than your father. Could it be that the request to attend Helen's parents' Christmas dinner reminded you of your absence from your own parents on this family occasion?

I remember the Christmas day when I received the gift of the German howitzer I had avidly looked at in the toy shop. Mother had observed how much I wanted it and bought it for me, even though it was more than she could afford.

T: You knew that your mother loved you.

I remember her disappointment when I could not take up the scholarship because she could not afford the uniform. I felt that I had failed her.

*

In the next session, he says to T:

I could predict that every year I would be subjected to Helen's insistence on the Christmas dinner, but I could not have predicted her announcement that she intended teaching art classes at the CAE in the evening one or two nights a week. When I asked her what she wanted to do that for, she said it was to pay for the children's high school uniforms which were beyond her skills on the sewing machine. I said that it was demeaning to teach at a place like the CAE. It was just housewives who wanted to get out of the house, and besides, we didn't need the money.

I assumed that would be the end of it but a few days later she asked me to sign a form confirming her credentials as an artist given my authority as an art master at Melbourne Grammar. Naturally I refused. A minute later I heard her speaking on the telephone and then I heard the back door open and close as she left the house, presumably to get a signature from whoever it was on the phone.

As I walked down the hallway, the sight of the scholarship painting took me back to that moment when the winner was announced. I knew then what I must do. I grabbed the painting at the two sides and raised it up to detach the wires from the picture hooks. There was no time to appreciate the little comedy of the hooks spontaneously dancing to the floor. I took a box of matches from the stove, picked up *The Herald* and with one hand holding the painting and the other holding the matches and the newspaper, I pushed open the back door with my foot and steered the painting towards the backyard incinerator. After tossing in a few pages of the newspaper, I threw in a match. I then ripped the canvas from the frame, snapped the frame into pieces with my foot, crumpled up the canvas, held it over the fire in an unceremonious farewell, then allowed it to fall into the burning incinerator. I watched as the flames licked their way over the formative work of my career, dissolving into ashes.

I went inside, poured myself a drink and sat in front of the television before going to bed early to avoid Helen's triumphant return with the recently acquired signature.

The next morning, the blank wall announced the deed committed in the backyard incinerator. When Helen asked me what had happened to the scholarship painting, I told her that I had burnt it, that it was my painting, I could do what I liked with it.

The painting was never referred to again until years later when Sasha Grishin asked to see it for a book he was writing on my work. I told him that I had burnt it as an inferior student work. Helen did not contradict me.

T: You told me that you considered burning the painting in your fury at not getting the scholarship. Helen had vehemently protested. Could it be that the actual burning of the painting was vengeance against Helen for taking a teaching job for a few nights a week?

It was my own fault. If I had not burnt the painting it would have been hung in my retrospective exhibition. It would have proved to be a formative work which should have won the Travelling Scholarship.

T: It would be vindication for not winning the prize you felt you justly deserved.

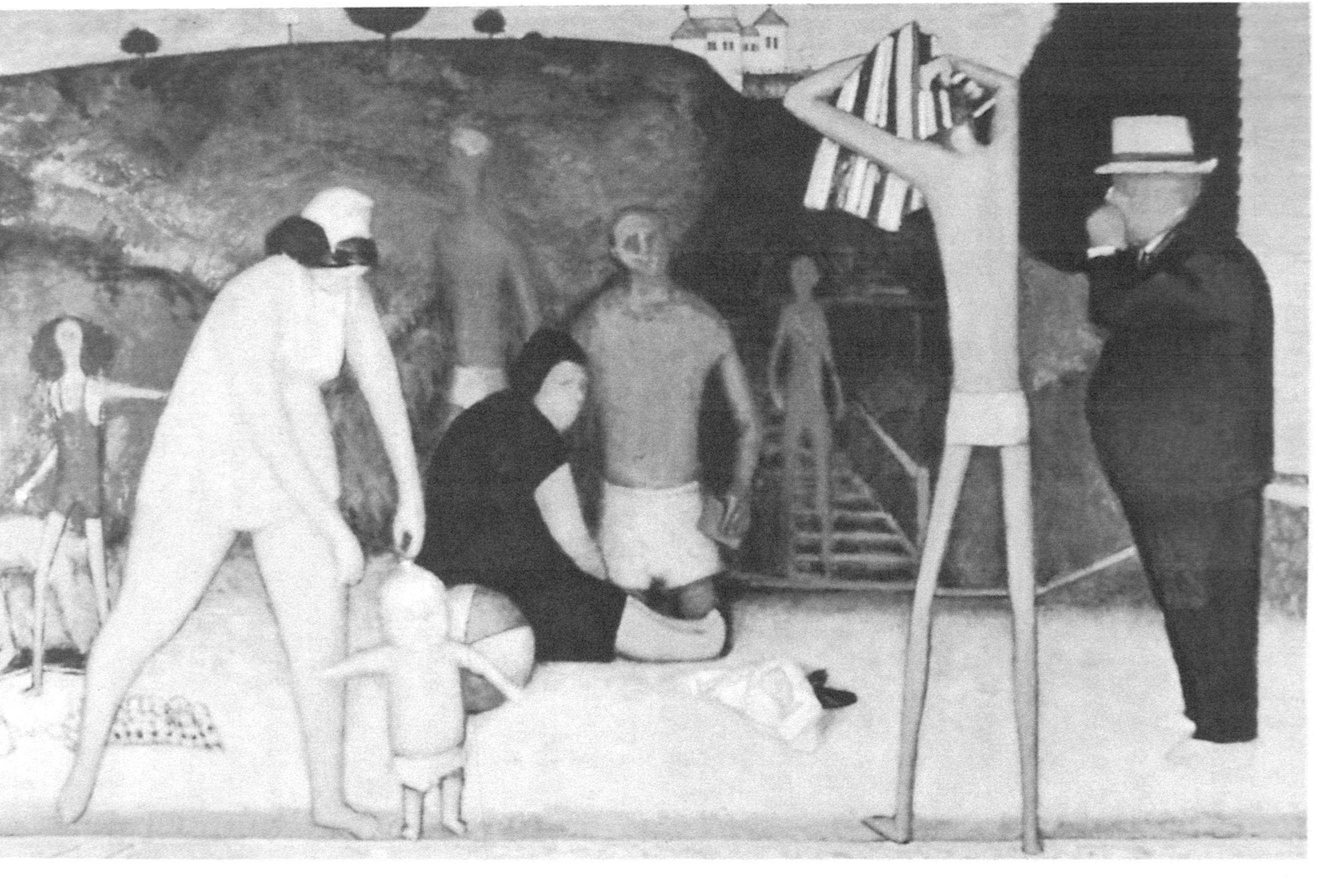

John Brack, *The Beach* 1949, oil on canvas 104.1 × 154.9 cm signature details unknown.

Mum taught evening and weekend classes at the CAE for over forty years. Often at a gallery opening, a former student would approach her and tell her how much they valued her classes, how much they had learned.

He tells T:

Helen would only earn a pittance teaching at the CAE but it struck me in the middle of the night that if she could get a job, she might leave me. Many years later when Mac took an interest in Helen's work, another fear took hold of me.

Mac and Jessie had come to lunch. After spending an hour looking at my paintings, I heard Mac ask Helen about her recent work. Enthusiastically she showed Mac her paintings while I was left with the tedious task of filling in time entertaining Jessie.

That evening Helen was noticeably buoyed up by the attention from Mac. Apparently, he had suggested putting titles on her work. 'You already have titles,' I said. He suggested longer titles that said more about what she had told him in explaining her work.

T: What was so disconcerting about Mac's interest in Helen's work?

Mac was my friend. I had never entered Helen's painting room. I had never talked to her about her work. That night I lay in bed allowing my mind to play tricks on me. What if Helen became successful? What if others took an interest in her work?

The next day at breakfast time I was jolted out of the fear that Helen's success would eclipse my own. Helen's paintings were erudite, oblique, not easily accessible. She was an artist's artist. Besides, she did not have the support of gallery directors or anybody else for that matter. As Helen handed me the plate of poached eggs, I wondered how I could have allowed myself to sink into fear.

T: You are telling me that you needed Helen to support your career, but the support was not reciprocal.

Dad would probably say, 'That was her job,' but this time he doesn't.

He goes on:

In the 1950s, I painted a portrait of Helen. Forty years later I painted another portrait. She was in her early sixties. 'He has painted me as quite austere, quite severe,' I heard her saying to a visitor. 'The role he has given me is, *No means no.*'

A reviewer suggested that I had painted her as 'the lighthouse in the artist's darkest moments of creative despair'.

'I mean, I ask you!' she said. 'I've never heard of anything so ridiculous. A lighthouse.' She was not given to the metaphoric.

Helen was not so much a lighthouse, but a torch. Sometimes a flickering torch, sometimes a torch held with fury, sometimes an illuminating torch. If Helen was a torch, she was also a taskmaster. Her insistence that 'no means no' sent me back into the studio when I felt like giving up.

T: What would you have done without Helen?

How would I know how to tie my shoelaces?

T: You could not have done without her.

The doctor tells me I would have drunk myself to death if Helen had not provided me with dinners of meat, potatoes and three vegetables every night.

T: Are you telling me that you are grateful to Helen for keeping you alive?

Well, that was her job. I depended on her.

T: Thank you does not come naturally to you.

If 'thank you' does not come naturally to me, it came all too readily to Helen. It embarrassed me when her thanks to a waiter or a nurse were so profuse as to be condescending. Often they were spoken as the obligatory response. I remember her thank you when I gave her a large bottle of expensive French perfume for her birthday. A week later during an argument I reminded her of it.

'What rot,' she said. 'You think that's a present! It's just guilt, guilt about the whiskey you buy yourself. It's the same colour. It's in a glass bottle.' She was right.

I *have* been known to say thank you. Following Helen's directives, I have made the odd phone call, written the odd thank you letter.

T: If Helen instructed you to write a thank you letter to others, she could hardly instruct you to thank herself.

That didn't stop her seeing thanks where they were not intended. In my last painting there are five figures, a larger one and four smaller ones. Helen sees these five figures as herself and the children. She sees this as my acknowledgement for all that she and the children had done for my work. 'It was the nicest thing John ever did,' she said. She found what she was looking for in the painting.

T: You took Helen for granted.

I could not have painted without Helen. I could not imagine another woman fulfilling the role as splendidly as she did. No other person would have had her diligence, her understanding of art, her desire for my success even more than her own.

T: What was so difficult about thanking Helen yourself?

It would have been demeaning. It would have been admitting that I could not have done it on my own.

Silence.

I did once think about it.

T: You thought about it.

We had gone shopping for a Persian rug required for painting a portrait. I expected to find one at the first shop we visited but none materialised like the one I had in mind. In my annoyance that our task was taking far longer than I had anticipated, I found myself engulfed with frustration, irritated with Helen's driving, with the rigmarole of parking the car and finding another shop.

Eventually I agreed on a rug simply for the sake of giving up on looking. When we arrived home, I remarked to Helen that it was a whole day away from painting. It was a whole day away from her painting, too, she said. It didn't matter to her one way or the other whether I found the rug I was looking for. I was the one who was looking. I was the one who was getting increasingly disappointed. She was merely doing the driving.

On the evening walk I thought that perhaps I would say thank you to Helen. As she said, she had given up a day of her own work to help buy the rug that I needed for my work. I said to myself that when I returned, I would say thank you. I stepped from the evening light into the kitchen and poured myself a drink. In the familiarity of the habits of the room I could not find the words that I had rehearsed outside on the walk. Broodingly, I sat at the table waiting for my dinner to be served, half-heartedly responding to Helen's attempts at conversation.

T: Coming from the outside to the inside you could not find words to say what you had planned.

It occurs to me now that if Helen wanted me to say thank you for what she had done for my work, she also wanted me to say sorry for my drinking.

T: We cannot say thank you if we cannot find gratitude within us. We cannot say sorry if we are silenced by our shame.

Sorry, sorry, sorry.

In the next session he says to T:

This pettiness about saying thank you and sorry is a way of avoiding the more serious question.

T: What question is that?

Who am I if I am not an artist?

T: Who are you if you are not an artist?

If I am not actually painting, I am solving the problems of the work, waiting for the solution to fall into place. I remember sitting in Christ Church, South Yarra, listening to the eulogy for Helen's mother, pondering the problem of the current painting. When the solution occurred to me, I saw myself squeezing out of the narrow pew, running out of the church, getting a taxi and throwing myself into the studio. I am never just posting a letter. Even when I am walking the streets of Surrey Hills, I am thinking of the problems of the work. There you are. I have answered the question, 'Who am I when I am not an artist?' I am a figure in the suburban landscape.

He is a figure in my internal landscape.

One would not put one hand on Dad's arm offering sympathy. I never saw him put his arm around another person. A touch would cause him to flinch. His favourite painting was Rembrandt's *The Jewish Bride*.

He tells T:

I will always remember the first time I saw Rembrandt's painting *The Jewish Bride*. I was looking at the most marvellous painting I had ever seen. It's the relationship between the man and the woman. The man inclines his head towards the woman. One of his hands protectively touches her heart. The fingers of her hand gently touch his hand in what seems like affirmation. The man and woman are not looking at each other but we are witnessing this private moment between them. It is a superb arrangement of hands. It's the touch of the man's hand on the woman's heart, the touch of her hand on his hand. The woman offers no resistance to the touch. I remember the first time I saw the painting, gazing at the image, held in the aura of it.

T: In looking at the painting perhaps you were incorporating the tenderness into yourself.

Silence.

I don't know, but it did have a profound effect on me. In the mid-1950s I started on my own version of the bride and groom. I wanted to show how the wedding day is the only time two people are united as one. The next day they confront the practical decision of how to live together.

After numerous attempts I abandoned the painting. It was all wrong. Years later, when I was picking up the children's toys, I found a little leaflet from a cake-decorating set. I knew then what was needed in the painting. It needed the wedding cake.

I had attempted the painting in dark red, burnt orange and russet, the colours in *The Jewish Bride*, but now I realised that the twentieth-century wedding demanded pale pinks, blues and yellows as shown in the little leaflet of the cake-decorating set.

As one problem was solved another had arisen. The painting needed something else. The solution came as I glanced at the photos of the bride and groom in the social pages of the newspaper. Little flecks of white randomly dotted the black-and-white photos as if rain had spotted the photograph. I realised then that what the painting needed was confetti.

Painting is touch. The paintbrush touching the paint, the paint touching the canvas under the masterful eye of the artist. I am a master of touch. Never let it be said that I am a man fearful of touch. Look at the paintings.

Silence.

T: Silence is touch.

In the next session he tells T:

It seems to me that when most people look at a painting or a shop window, they see the object behind the glass. But when I look at something behind glass, the first thing I see is a reflection of myself.

I remember looking into a shop that sold chairs for invalids and other sorts of props for people with disabilities. My reflection on the glass superimposed itself over the proprietor and the lady assistant who seemed to be swimming in the middle of the shop. I was struck by the peculiarity of the relationship between the people inside and me outside looking in.

T: What was peculiar about the relationship?

It seemed to me that the proprietor and his assistant were almost disembodied in the way that I felt disembodied.

T: You felt cut off from yourself.

I painted another picture of a shop window where you see a manikin figure of a boy standing on an oversized wheelchair. One of his legs is an artificial leg. He is smiling because he is happy to have found the props that enable him to stand and to walk. The section of the painting where he stands is bathed in dramatic red.

T: If painting is touch, I wonder if touching the paint on canvas is a prop like the artificial leg for the boy. It's a prop connecting you to yourself. You become embodied when you are painting.

When I am painting, I become a happy boy.

The Happy Boy was painted mid-career. *Little Boy Lost* was painted early career.

*

Dad was on the lookout for what would solve the problem of the wedding pictures. I am on the lookout for what will explain how his conversations with T seem real. In the introduction to a collection of Italian folktales, Italo Calvino tells us: 'Now my journey through folklore is over...I know that this was not a hallucination, a sort of professional malady, but the confirmation of something I already suspected—folktales are real.'

In his journey through teaching the great Russian short stories, George Saunders tells us he discovered a sort of knowledge that is real but cannot be put into words. We can 'know' something but we cannot articulate what we know. The 'knowing' at such moments is real, even though it cannot be articulated.

What I do know is that my father's conversations with T are transformative. I cannot explain it. They are transformative for him and for me. They take the form of what we say when we say, 'I promise'. Something real happens in the exchanges between them.

*

He continues:

I once did a series of paintings of a wooden hand that artists use as a model for painting hands. I cannot recall how I got the idea to paint the articulated wooden hand except that I had seen one in an art supplies shop forty years before. In order to paint the hand, I needed a model. I went into the art material shop and was just about to ask the assistant if they had an articulated wooden hand, when I noticed that he had no right hand.

I then painted the hand into a shop window with postcards balanced on the fingers. I was drawn to painting shop windows and if not a window, a frame painted around the edge of the painting. This gives the impression that we are looking at the painting, outside looking in.

T: How did you get the idea for painting the shop window?

The idea for the shop window as a painting device came to me in 1962 when an image from my childhood rose unbidden in the night. It was the image of a window displaying hundreds of pocketknives and cutlery and that sort of thing. They were scattered higgledy-piggledy, as if they had been tossed in at random with no aesthetic sense of arrangement.

T: The image of the shop window had stayed with you since childhood.

It occurs to me now that the paintings of shop windows return me to that moment when I first saw the shop window with the Van Gogh print that had inspired me to paint.

T: The moment of the epiphany when you felt a tingling in the spine.

Albert Camus said, 'A person's life purpose is nothing more than to rediscover, through the detours of art or love or passionate work, those one or two images in the presence of which his heart first opened.' Although I am known as a cerebral painter, as a 'cool detached observer', it could be said that I am seeking to return to that moment when the heart first opened.

Dad remembers the shop that sold pocketknives and cutlery. I remember the paintings inspired by the shop he remembered from childhood.

He continues:

The Van Gogh that I had seen in the shop window was only a print. I was considered remiss for not travelling overseas to see the paintings in the original but our own gallery, the National Gallery of Victoria, had a modest collection of Picassos, Rembrandts, Seurats and Modiglianis. It was not until my early fifties that Helen and I planned our first trip overseas. Right from the beginning, Helen and I disagreed on the itinerary. At one point Helen said she would stay at home, and I would have to go alone. I said that if she didn't come, she would be depriving me of the paintings I had wanted to see all my life.

And then what should happen when we set off? Once in the aeroplane, Helen delighted in the little packaged meals delivered to her as I sunk into dejection at the sheer ordeal of the prospect of what was to follow.

T: So what was to follow?

On the first day as we waited outside the Louvre, I wondered if the whole thing was a mistake. At the designated time, the doors opened and the crowd surged forward as if their lives would be transformed by seeing great art. Unsettled by the unexpected crowds, I found myself yearning for my natural habitat, the studio. I remember looking at the Velasquez, thinking, 'Is it worth all the effort to get here?'

T: You had not anticipated the number of tourists.

I had expected the aura of the painting in the flesh, not the crowds of other tourists flocking to the gallery at the same time as we were. It was naïve of me to imagine that I would be looking at the paintings alone just because art was my profession. A 'great' gallery gives the paintings within it the mystique of Great Art. These tourists would not look twice if they saw the same paintings in a little gallery up a dead-end laneway. It was not just the bobbing of other people's heads in front of the painting, neither was it the subdued chatter...these large assemblies of *grand peintures* were hung as if they were proclaiming, 'Look at me. Look at me. I am a genius. I am a hero.' It is not the fault of the artist. It is the curators, the gallery directors and the critics who lift the finished work out of the mundane ordinariness of the artist's studio into the glitter of the Kingdom of Art.

Overwhelmed by the clamour of 'look at me', 'the artist as hero', I fled downstairs where I found the work of the Egyptians, Sumerians and Assyrians. There I had the opportunity to look at them intently without the encumbrance of other bodies and without the proclamations of the greatness of the work.

One would think that I would have learnt my lesson after the Louvre but the same thing happened when visiting the Rijksmuseum in Amsterdam. We had gone there to see *The Jewish Bride* but the enormity of the crowds sent me retreating downstairs to the basement. The silent dignity of the Buddhist statue *Guanyin Avolokiteshva* made *The Jewish Bride* look vulgar.

I had set out on the journey to look at the paintings only to discover the obstruction and the fascination with other people not looking at the paintings. Tourists flocked to the gift shops buying postcards of what they had not really seen. It's the existential dread. The need to have something in one's hand, a souvenir, something to show for it. I bought some of the postcards myself knowing I would do something with them, but not knowing what.

T: So the whole expedition did not fulfil what you had imagined it would.

To make things worse, right from the beginning it seemed that I was prepared to take a more leisurely approach than Helen. As she revelled in the galleries I was wishing to return to the familiarity of the studio. Exhausted by the crowds in front of the paintings, I suggested wandering the city as flâneurs. At first she objected but then as she came to marvel at the shops, the parks, the people, I just wanted to get back to the hotel.

T: Let me get this right. Helen didn't want to go on the overseas expedition but you said you wouldn't go without her. When she agreed to come, she enjoyed it and you sulked at the ordeal. Instead of being gratified that Helen had found enjoyment in the trip you had manipulated her into taking, you punished her for her enjoyment as a disgruntled, surly travelling companion.

He says nothing.

Instead of succumbing to disappointment at his trip overseas, Dad did something imaginatively with the postcards he had bought. He copied them into his paintings, balancing them on knives and forks. He asked the three grandchildren to paint a picture of a king or queen on a blank postcard he had given them. He then painted their postcards in the same composition as the postcards of kings and queens painted by the great masters.

On returning from their trip overseas, Mum told me that when they were in Paris Uncle Lindsay had rung to tell Dad that their mother had died.

'How did Daddy respond to hearing of his mother's death?' I asked.

'Well, it was nothing really.'

'He must have felt sad or sorry or something.'

'No, he didn't. John wasn't like that.'

'He wasn't like what?'

'He wasn't sentimental.'

In my last year at school, we read *The Outsider* by Albert Camus translated from the French. It starts with, 'Mother died today. Or maybe it was yesterday, I don't know.'

In the next session he says to T:

I didn't tell you what else happened on that trip overseas. On the late afternoon of our third day in Paris, I returned to the hotel room while Helen did some shopping. I was glad to have the time alone but this meant that when the telephone rang it was incumbent on me to pick it up. I allowed it to ring, thinking it would stop, but when it continued, I answered, expecting the hotel receptionist. It was Lindsay speaking from the other side of the world. My ears must have been deceiving me, I thought, or someone was playing a trick on me or I must have been dreaming.

'Mother died today,' he said.

A guttural cry escaped me.

'I thought you should know,' Lindsay said, as if apologising for interrupting what he would have considered a holiday.

I offered to return for the funeral, knowing he would not expect me to return. After putting down the phone I stumbled to the armchair and sat down staring at the rosy patterned wallpaper, amused by the little comedy of hearing of Mother's death from inside a forest of tiny rosebuds. Shortly after, Helen returned.

'I just met this marvellous man and I bought this divine cheese and...'

'Mother died today,' I said. 'I don't remember whether Lindsay said "today" or "yesterday"; besides, the time difference would mean that if it was today here, it would be yesterday there or vice versa.'

In niggling over the day of Mother's death, I was avoiding what I didn't want to face: the fact of Mother's death. I wanted to be alone.

I told Helen I wanted to go out for a walk to the little park several blocks along the street. I stepped from the hotel and walked along the street comforted that I would not run into anyone I knew. I reached the park and sat down on one of the impractical little decorative chairs where I replayed Lindsay's words, 'Mother died today.' Time took on a new dimension. The sky turned a darker shade of blue, people were returning from work or going out for the evening. Every one of these human beings has a mother, I thought. Every one of these human beings loves and hates his mother.

As I sat there in the evening light, I found myself rummaging through memories of Mother. I remembered the toy gun from Father Christmas, knowing that Mother had found the money for it even though she could not afford it. I remembered sitting at the kitchen table doing my homework while Mother did the ironing. I remembered flinging words in her direction, 'vicarious', 'desultory', 'decrepitude', 'elucidate', knowing she would not know the meaning.

I remembered Mother's pride when I won the scholarship to Ivanhoe Grammar and her subsequent disappointment that she could not afford the uniform for me to go there. I remembered feeling protective of Mother at the excruciating engagement party where Helen's mother talked about the difficulty of getting good 'help'. I remembered Mother's delight when her first grandchild was born, a girl she had always wanted. I remembered the last time I spoke to Mother. It was on the phone. Neither of us said goodbye.

As I retraced my steps along the boulevard, I determined not to be lured into talking about Mother, knowing Helen's justifiable hostility to her. She was my mother.

I returned to the hotel room where Helen had arranged the divine cheese on a sheet of butcher's paper and had somehow procured a knife. Earlier that day we had looked at Manet's *Lunch on the Grass*. Now we were actually having dinner in a forest of rosebuds, inwardly absorbed in vastly different worlds, unknown to the other.

The next day as we entered the Galerie Orsay, I realised that outwardly everything looked the same—the queues outside the gallery, the cars driving around Paris. Yet something had irrevocably changed inside me.

T: Talking about your mother's death has revived your love and hate for your mother.

*

Dad was inventively confident in his paintings but he was not so confident in the practical tasks of dealing with his children. One Saturday morning when Mum was out shopping, I tumbled and fell from my bike. Blood trickled from a cut on my leg but I managed to get back on my bike and ride home. I intended to clean the wound myself, but Dad happened to be leaving the bathroom as I went in. 'I fell off my bike,' I said, explaining why I was entering the bathroom as he was leaving. I sat on the edge of the bath while Dad frantically searched in the medicine cupboard for a bandage. I probably said sorry for the trouble I was causing, taking him away from painting.

There is no reason for him to remember the experience, but if he does, this is how he reports it to T:

One morning when Helen was out shopping, one of the children rushed into the bathroom, blood dripping from her leg. She had fallen from her bike, she said. The sight of blood trickling from her leg threw me into a panic. Helplessly, I opened the medicine cupboard, only to be confronted by a jumbled forest of medicine bottles, pills and cotton-wool. Having found the bandage, I discovered it was in one long piece requiring a pair of scissors to cut it shorter. Helen had done nothing so sensible as to have the scissors nearby, so I scurried into our bedroom to her sewing machine and hunted around the mess of fabrics and pins to locate her dressmaking scissors. Eventually I managed to cut a bandage and then, having fumblingly dabbed the wound with mercurochrome, I placed the bandage over the open wound and then relocated everything into the cabinet as best I could. With the relief of one who no longer has to sing a song he doesn't know the words to, I escaped into the studio.

T: You escaped into the studio.

I was escaping from having to do something I was not practised in doing.

T: You were escaping from the ordeal of finding a bandage and putting it on a child's wound.

I was escaping the flesh and blood. Painting is my flesh and blood.

Long silence.

There was one other time when I felt compelled to escape into the studio.

T: What were you seeking to escape?

The grief over Freddy's death. I have often replayed the moment I heard that Freddy had cancer and not long to live. He was only fifty-four. His wife Lynn and three teenage daughters were losing a husband and father, but I was losing my closest friend.

Immediately after Freddy's death I wrote the eulogy for his funeral. I remember saying, 'The death of the artist is different from the death of others. While he lives the artist is his work, and when he dies, he stays behind. This is the great consolation both to the artist and to those who are left. The artist is his work.'

For me, the work was not sufficient consolation. Helen and the children wisely knew not to refer to Freddy's death. Nothing was spoken in the family until six months later on Christmas day. After dinner the children chatted innocuously as I sat there glumly until called upon to speak. Then, out of this cacophony, I heard Freddy's name. The children were speaking their reminiscences. They recalled how he gave them chocolate Freddo frogs when he was babysitting, how Freddy and I once played shuttlecock in the back garden much to their amusement. Then, after a lull in the reminiscences, a peculiar sound emerged from the footstool where the first daughter was sitting at the end of my chair. I assumed it was laughter about something she remembered of Freddy but then I realised it was the sound of weeping. A grown-up daughter sobbing, right there on the little footstool near my feet.

Instinctively I rose from my chair and left the room but after fetching more ice for the whiskey there was nowhere to sit. I could not return to my chair so near to this weeping, so I had no alternative but to roam the hallway restlessly, putting my head in the doorway repeating to no one in particular, 'Why is Clara crying? Freddy was my friend.'

By the time they were leaving she had recovered from her weeping. Usually, I hover in the background hoping to avoid the perfunctory kiss but this time I found myself lurching towards the weeping daughter, throwing my arms around her, grasping her to me as tightly as all my strength permitted. After letting go, she stared at me speechless, gasping for breath. I do not know what overcame me.

T: You could not weep at the death of your dearest friend so your daughter took it on herself to do the weeping for you. The attempt at embrace was your attempt at acknowledgement.

I do not know if that is the explanation. Nothing was ever spoken of it. I remember thinking for half a second that Dad was coming to give me a hug, but the hug turned out to be an almost suffocation.

Another memory of tears returns to me. This time I was trying to conceal the tears. I was six or seven years old. Dad was drawing my portrait. I was trying with all my effort to sit perfectly still, thinking that if I moved, he would make a mistake. He must have noticed my tears for I remember him saying, 'You can move, you know.'

Nearly thirty years later, he did portraits of the four of us daughters. Mum had gone overseas. He refused to go with her. I remember preparing for the sitting thinking, 'I will not see him as the omnipotent father. I will not see him as the observer like the man on the beach in the scholarship painting.' I remember composing myself respectfully, sitting on the chair looking at him a few feet away, his pencil sketching lines on his drawing pad. As I watched him look at me, put the pencil on the paper, drawing a line, it occurred to me that's all a portrait is, one pencil line after another.

After the sitting I helped him put together the lunch. Mum always managed the conversation so now that she wasn't here it was up to me to ask Dad questions about art. It never occurred to me to tell him what was going on in my life. I do remember him taking a Nabokov novel from his bookshelf, 'You might like this,' he said. I took this as an offer to connect.

A professional photographer took several photographs of Dad sitting in the studio with the portraits behind him. We were shown the set of photographs and asked to select one. Later I regretted not picking a photograph that was more characteristic of him. I had chosen one of him smiling as I had imagined the photographer had instructed.

He says to T:

I had drawn pictures of the children when they were very young. I named the pictures *First Daughter, Second Daughter, Third Daughter* and *Fourth Daughter*. When Helen went overseas one summer holiday, I drew portraits of them again, now they were in their thirties. This time I gave them their names, *Portrait of Clara/Vicky/Freda* and *Charlotte*.

T: You chose the time to do the portraits when Helen was overseas.

It would give me some connection with them without Helen's interference.

I remember drawing each daughter's head, doing the chit-chat required for anyone sitting for their portrait. I remember sketching in one daughter's eyes realising that I knew very little about her. I knew more about my students at the art school. The relief when she left was like when any sitter left. Now I could get on with my real work back in the studio. This time the relief was accompanied by the sense of having missed something.

T: What had you missed?

That moment of drawing their portraits would never be repeated. That is the closest I will ever get to my children. I knew nothing about girls. I had one brother. It's not just that they were girls. How could I get to know them? I was busy in the studio. Never did we do anything so much as toss a ball between us. Our paths crossed as we went in or out of a room. When they were little, they were more like encumbrances. Their toys were strewn around the floor and when they were older there was the petty bickering, and then their miseries that didn't concern me. How could I have a conversation with any one of them given their ignorance about the world?

Then there were the tantrums and Helen's petty worries about them, worries that she attempted to inflict onto me and which I satisfactorily avoided. Maybe none of us know our children. Did Tolstoy know his children? How could he get to know his children if he was writing *War and Peace*?

Long silence.

My children have grown up with my paintings on the walls. They know me from the paintings. I may not know very much about them, but they know me in a way that I do not know myself.

I had always understood that we didn't see much of Dad because he was so busy painting, but it wasn't until Mum's response to our time with him in hospital that I wondered if there was another reason for our distance from our father.

He was in hospital recovering from a prostate operation. The nurses could not be expected to sit with a patient with dementia so

Mum drew up a roster for the four of us to take turns sitting with him when she could not be there herself. It required holding him back from pulling at the catheter, stopping him from wrestling his way out of the hospital gown, explaining that he was in hospital, not in a hotel preparing to give a speech. It required thinking up a topic that might inspire conversation.

When Mum arrived at 10.30 pm ready to take over for the night, I was eager to get home but she demanded that I stay. She wanted to demonstrate her caring technique, proving its superiority to mine. Stroking Dad's face she repeated, 'It's all right lambie pie, I am here. There, there lambie pie.' The bleak desperation of the repeated 'lambie pie' was unbearable.

Another time I had only just arrived when she told me that my face was lopsided, one side looking swollen. She wondered whether I had cancer. I understood the stress of looking after Dad, the anger at seeing him with dementia, the responsibility of caring for him with barely a moment to herself—but why would she create anxiety in me suggesting I had cancer when I was only trying to help?

Mum had no choice but to roster us to look after Dad. Her reaction wasn't sympathetically, 'I know how hard it is. It must be confronting seeing your father in this state.' It was, 'There you all are, swanning in to see your father.' As she saw it, we were not rushing to the hospital from the other side of town after work in peak-hour traffic having grabbed something for dinner. We were 'swanning in'.

Over the years I had gleaned that Mum longed to have some meaningful connection with *her* father but now I wondered whether she may have felt threatened if we had some connection with our own.

After Dad's death, I offered my condolences, sympathising with Mum's loss, knowing her struggle looking after him. I acknowledged her grief. She conveyed no sense that I had 'lost' a father, not that he was a wonderful father, but he *was* my father. The mourning was all hers. He belonged to her.

When Mum suggested that we were swanning in to see our father, the phrase 'swanning in' suggested that perhaps there was another story about Dad's distance from us children. Perhaps it was not Dad who wanted to be kept away from his children; perhaps it was Mum who would rather we not have a relationship with our father. 'Swanning in' suggested an Oedipal attachment, 'courting' our father. I did a quick sort through my memories of our experience with Dad to see if I could identify any other clues as confirmation.

Dad chose to do our portraits when Mum was overseas. When I overheard him saying to Mum, 'Of course I am only doing the children's portraits as practice for Ursula,' I was hurt. Weren't we worthy of having our portraits drawn, just in being his daughters? Perhaps he was reassuring Mum that he didn't really want to spend time with us, it was all just practice for a more important person.

I recall the Christmas dinner when Mum went overseas. We usually have the dinner in the dining room. This time Dad set up a long trestle table in his studio. He had cooked the meal himself with some considerable assistance. He was actually smiling and seemed pleased with himself for making us this offer. We were in his territory, the studio. I remember the Christmas decorations around the room.

'There you are, swanning in to see your father.' I wondered if Mum feared we had the same attachment to Dad that she had. She is the wife. We are the children. Art was their joint work together.

I can hear Mum saying, 'No, that's just rubbish.'

The next session he says to T:

After more than a decade teaching at Melbourne Grammar, I was asked to be head of the National Gallery art school, the school where I had studied. I said that I would only do it if I had a studio and only for a few years until they could find a more permanent replacement.

In the first week after starting work I walked through the city, glancing in the shop windows reorienting myself, when I found myself staring at a display of pens. I decided to buy an expensive fountain pen which I could now afford with the full-time salary I was earning.

I selected a wine-red pen with gold trimming. The shop assistant demonstrated how to fill it and then handed me a writing pad on which were scrawled the cursive scripts of others before me, *Carpe diem, The rain in Spain stays mainly on the plain, Happy birthday.* I made my contribution *Garlic and sapphires in the mud.* The shop assistant then produced a box with gold trimming lined with royal-blue velvet. He placed the pen into the groove, shutting the box with a silent thud. He then asked if it was a gift and when I said no, he put it into a brown paper bag.

A year later the question, 'Is it a gift?' returned when my first daughter left school and was about to go to university. I had been thinking of buying her a gift as a rite of passage. Helen organised the presents for birthdays and Christmas, so this was my opportunity to assert myself as a father.

I went into the shop and selected the same pen as the one I had bought myself. The shop assistant put it into its blue velvet crib and when he asked if it was a gift, I assured him that indeed it was. I now had the opportunity to observe him meticulously wrapping the box in gold-and-red-striped wrapping paper, completing the performance with the flourish of a red bow.

When I got home, I put the parcel on the coffee table. There was something not quite right about the wrapping paper. The exquisite, careful wrapping looked uncharacteristic of something I would give. I undid the bow and then proceeded to rip off the wrapping paper, knowing that in two seconds I had wrecked what the fellow in the shop had taken five minutes to perfect.

I then opened the box and gazed at the fountain pen. The royal-blue velvet box gave it a regal pretension, more like a gift Helen's family would give. I lifted out the pen and held it in my hand. It was gleamingly new, not marked with little scratches like my own.

A few hours later, my daughter came into the room where I was sitting alone. I put down the book I was reading, swivelled around to the bookshelf behind me, grabbed the pen and thrust it in her direction, hearing myself say, 'Take this. I bought it for myself. I don't use it anymore. You might as well have it. And take this ink,' I added, handing over the unopened bottle.

The effusiveness of her thanks was noticeably greater than was warranted for something I had bought for myself and didn't use anymore.

T: After your good intentions you thrust the pen at your daughter as if it was any old thing you no longer needed, a cast-off.

I knew then why I wanted to give this gift. I had not received a gift like this from my father. Leaving school at fifteen and a half was not a cause for celebration; it was a rebuke to my father for not being able to afford to keep me at school, especially since my teachers had urged me to stay for my academic potential. Keeping my children at school was a sign of my success as a father.

T: You wanted to give your daughter what your father did not give to you, but because he had not given it to you, your resentment stopped you from giving it with the generosity with which it was intended.

For the very reason that my father did not give me a gift on leaving school, I wanted to give one to my daughter. But because he had not given me this gift, I did not know how to give it.

Fifteen years after handing over the pen, I received a letter from my daughter, scolding me for what she saw as my negligence as a father. She drew attention to the fact that the letter was written with the fountain pen I had claimed that I no longer needed. I replied to her letter with the pen that I had bought for myself.

Two days after posting the letter, I noticed an envelope addressed to my husband in my father's handwriting. 'Why is he writing to Ross?' I wondered. I looked again. It was addressed to 'Mrs Ross Williams'.

My father had addressed the envelope to me in my husband's name. I had also written a letter to my mother and a joint letter to both of them.

Dad wrote back suggesting that I was 'troubled' and if there was anything to do to help, he would. Many years later, when he was in hospital with dementia, he told me that the doctor had written a letter to Mum. 'Oh,' I said, 'what did it say?'

He glared at me. 'It was like that letter you wrote to me, so *scolding*.'

In the many hours of crafting the letter, I thought I had concealed my anger at him. I reread my copy of it. He was right. It was scolding.

He tells T about my letter:

One day, unexpectedly, I received a letter from my first daughter. I read the letter once, just enough to get the gist of it. When I realised she was roughly the same age as I was when I painted *The Return of the Prodigal Son*, I knew then that the letter was not for me, it was for her. It was for her to express her anger at me for my failings as a father.

Helen had also received a letter. I had no inclination to tell her what was in mine and presumed that her letter expressed the same incriminating disappointment.

After some fussing about, wanting to tell me and avoiding what she wanted to tell me, Helen told me what she didn't want to tell me. A stranger had taken our daughter to the creek bed at the bottom of the hill where we lived. He had raped her.

I could not bear to think about it. The brutality of men in the army upset me. As a boy I could not tolerate fights in the school yard. I wanted to banish the thought from my mind. A rape was too awful to contemplate. I did the sums. I told Helen that by my calculation, it happened almost twenty-five years ago, plenty of time to get over it.

I returned to the studio somewhat rattled. After three attempts at painting, I put down the paintbrush, washed the brushes and walked up the street intending to buy another bottle of whiskey in case I ran out. I needed to find a way of dealing with Helen's response. She would blame herself, 'I tried so hard to do the right thing.' She would blame our daughter, 'Why didn't she tell us before?' She would berate herself, 'I told the children over and over never to speak to strange men.'

On the way home from the bottle shop, I considered how to deal with Helen's response. I knew she would not let it go. On arriving back home, I scurried over to the shadows under the tree near the back fence, wondering how to tell Helen that I didn't want to know what happened any more than she did. I dug up the leaves with my bare hands, making a shallow grave for the whiskey bottle and as I rumpled the leaves, concealing the bottle, the thought came to me, 'It didn't happen.' The problem of Helen's distress had been solved.

I returned to the studio repeating to myself, 'It didn't happen, it didn't happen.'

With renewed energy, I focused on painting for the remainder of the afternoon. At 5 pm I paused at the flywire door, rehearsing my declaration. When I stepped inside the kitchen, I was surprised to see Helen holding a glass vase, swivelling a tea towel into the centre of it in a way I had never seen before. 'It didn't happen,' I said. After a few back-and-forth remarks about whether it did or did not happen, we let the matter rest. The next morning, Helen had come to her senses. It was never mentioned again.

T: Do you believe that your daughter was raped?

She could not have made it up. She wasn't prone to telling lies. I could not bear to think about it.

T: In telling Helen that it hadn't happened you were telling her that you were not willing to listen to her concerns about it.

My exhibition was in two months.

In the year of the rape, Dad painted *The Chase*, a painting of three of us children running. I remember the dresses. Granny, Mum's mother, bought them from Georges. Mum didn't like the Peter Pan collars so close to the neck, so she cut them off with the scissors, scooping out the necks.

In the next session he says to T:

I do not know why my daughter felt she had to tell Helen what happened at the creek bed. When we wrote letters home from the army, we protected our parents from what distressed us. We put it all behind us. No soldier would consider telling his parents what happened when he returned home.

T: So what did happen in the army?

The humiliation of the first night in the army jolted me into seeing how ill-prepared I was for the company of men. My literacy and aptitude for maths meant that I was rapidly promoted. It was my job to hand out the letters from home. One day in the silence after distributing the letters, I happened to look up from reading my own letter when I noticed a fellow glancing towards me, one of the fellows who had mocked me for my poetry books, threatening to tear it to pieces. I knew then what he wanted. I motioned him to follow me outside, and it was there behind the mess hall that I read aloud the letter from his girlfriend, and it was there the next day that he dictated his letter in response.

Not all letters from wives and girlfriends expressed the same devotion. One day the quiet reading was shattered by the sound of a gunshot. A soldier had shot himself in the head. Only moments before, I had handed him his letter. Instinctively, I found myself reading the open pages he had left. His fiancé had written to tell him she was very sorry, but she was marrying another man.

T: It was not your fault. There was nothing you could have done to prevent it.

It's the futility of his death. He was only twenty-one, a boy. It was the futility of war. It was the wastefulness of life, not just his life but all those whose lives were lost by the killing in war. We weren't even fighting in battle. We were soldiers in training. I couldn't bear it.

T: Who knows what else was going on in the life of that young man? Who knows what other troubles he carried from his childhood? It was not your fault.

Who knows what other troubles my father carried from his childhood? He told me about the shooting in the army but there must be other traumas he did not tell. I invent a single event that represents all that he kept hidden.

He says to T:

One morning when I was still a schoolboy, I noticed a brown paper bag concealed in the privet hedge near the front fence. It appeared to have been shoved into the hedge by someone passing in the street as if posted anonymously into the hedge instead of the letterbox. Curious to know what was in it, I pulled it out and opened it up but then closed it. I looked again. I didn't want to know. I put it back where I found it. I continued walking to school, wondering if I had really seen what I had seen. I thought I had done something wrong, but I didn't know what it was.

All day the image reappeared before me. A newborn or not-yet-born baby, dead. I could not understand how it had got there. I remembered overhearing Mother saying something about Mrs Jelbart over the road having had a 'backyard abortion'. I understood it was wrong. I wondered if the baby was something to do with an 'abortion'.

I was frightened. I thought I should tell someone, but there was no one I could tell. When I got back home, the paper bag had gone. I could pretend to myself that I had never seen it but I knew that I had.

T: You saw something you didn't understand. You kept that knowledge to yourself. You connected to the fear that you had done something wrong but didn't know what it was.

I did not understand what made me conjure up this image to represent what I did not know about Dad's childhood. It did not seem like something that would happen.

Another memory came back to me. Mum told us that she had given birth to twins very prematurely. All I knew was that they died.

He tells T:

Nine months after Freda was born, Helen became pregnant with twins, a girl and a boy. They both died, born prematurely.

T: That must have been very distressing, especially for Helen.

She didn't talk about it.

T: As you had not talked about that glimpse of the baby in the paper bag, Helen had not talked about the death of the twins. As you had no experience of being listened to, you had no capacity to listen to Helen.

You are listening to me. I am listening to myself. Hand on my heart.

*

I am wondering where to go from here. I started with the intention of finding compassion for my father. I had hoped it was compassion for him that stopped me from taking the photograph of him on our Sunday walk. I remembered a story told by the writer James Ellroy. The detectives had botched the investigation into the murder of his mother, so he decided to take a break from writing to do his own investigation. Some time into his investigation, he realised that it wasn't his mother's murderer he needed to find. He needed to find out about his mother's life before she was so brutally taken from him.

My intention was to find compassion for my father. Perhaps my real need is for *him* to find compassion for his mother.

As far as I know, Dad made no attempt to contact his mother and she made no attempt to contact him. Surely a mother would long to see her child before she died. I remembered Maria who was in the hospital bed next to mine.

I give my experience of Maria to my father.

He tells T:

Last week I was in hospital for a routine procedure. Maria was in the bed next to mine. 'Why she not come? Why she not come?' she called after pressing the button for the nurse. I assured her that the nurse would come when she was ready.

At visiting hours Maria's daughter arrived and I could hear mother and daughter conversing in Greek, more like bickering than a conversation. After a long, expressive monologue from Maria, followed by a brief reply from her daughter, the daughter emerged from behind the blue curtain.

'She is driving me mad. I'm not coming to see her again.'

After the daughter left, I thought I should say something to Maria, if for no other reason than to let her know that the monologue had interrupted my reading.

'So that was Toula, your daughter,' I said.

'Yes,' said Maria, and then her voice raised to a kind of bleating, 'But why he not come? Why he not come?' Thinking she had got her pronouns mixed up, I told her the nurse would come when she was ready. It wasn't the nurse she wanted. It was her son. 'Peter, my son. Why he not come?' It was pitiful, a grown woman calling for her son.

T: You saw Maria and you saw your mother longing to see you.

If that is how the mother speaks to her daughter, the son has the good sense not to see her.

The next day the blue curtain was pulled back to reveal Maria sitting on the bed ready to go home. She was dressed in a nondescript skirt and a grey windcheater imprinted with a large pink heart. A man almost twice her size arrived and, without looking at her, mumbled a few words in Greek as he picked up her suitcase. In his floor-length billowing black dress and heavy silver cross dangling around his neck, he majestically led the way with Maria behind him—a frail creature grasping her handbag in one hand and the red carnations her daughter had given her in another.

'Goodbye Maria,' I said. 'I wish I was going home.'

T: You saw the disdain in the priest and you saw yourself. You are seeking to find compassion for your mother. You are seeking to find compassion for yourself.

I want to believe that he is able to hear what T is saying. But then what does he do? He flees the scene of the revelation as if it was a crime he had committed. It is too much for him to take in.

In the next session he says to T:

I don't know why I am here. I know now that I am not mad although I have always feared insanity. I should be back in the studio, painting. Helen will be wondering where I am. She probably has the dinner ready for me.

T: This is your response to my suggestion that you are seeking to find compassion for your mother, compassion for yourself.

When I was at the gallery school, my secretary came in offering her unsolicited opinion on the painting I was doing. 'I suppose your experiences in the war make you paint like that,' she said. 'I was just as morbid before the war,' I said.

I am still morbid. I don't know the origin and even if I did, I wouldn't tell you. I may be morbid, but I am not mad. What is it with all this talking? It is pure self-indulgence. And besides, it's not as if you are telling me truths about the world like Heidegger's theory of being. There is nothing more you can extract from me. If I was going to do a picture of this, I would call it *Nothing. Nothing to be done*. I have finished. Is man no more than this? No, I have a better idea. I will call it *Exit*. Time for my departure. Time to end these sessions. I am leaving.

T: Let us continue for another four weeks as a transition to ending our sessions.

Four weeks will be more than sufficient.

The next session he comes in hobbling on crutches, his leg in plaster. He says to T:

As you can see, I have broken my leg. I stumbled and fell into a pothole in the pavement.

T: Just as you are thinking of leaving our sessions you repeat the act that led you here in the first place.

I used to be fascinated by a single artificial leg in a shop window I passed as a student on the way to the gallery school. As far as I could see, there was nothing else in the shop but every time I passed the window, I saw a man peeping out. I never failed to look in the window and he never failed to look out.

Twenty years later when I returned to the gallery school, I tried to find the shop, but it was no longer there. It had been replaced by another surgical supply shop nearby. I knew that I must paint the more recent shop window, but before that I would paint the memory of the window that had left such a strong impression on me.

T: What was it about the single artificial leg that had left such a strong impression on you?

The single prosthetic leg in the shop window presented itself like an object in a museum. I was influenced by the French philosopher André Malraux who wrote *The Museum Without Walls*. The single prosthetic leg represented the existential terror of the individual seeking purpose in life. It amused me to imagine a man hobbling along on one leg and passing the shop window, saying ecstatically, 'That is just what I wanted.' Originally, I called the painting *Artificial Limb-maker's Shop* but when I realised I had inadvertently solved the problem of the cliché of the still life of the bowl of fruit and flowers, I renamed it *Still Life with Artificial Leg*.

See! he says, pointing to his leg. This is *Still Life with Plastered Leg*. Or *Leg Stilled in Plaster*.

T laughs.

The leg appeared to me as a lost object, a leg looking for a companion leg, a dancer looking for the dance. When I put the finishing touches on the anonymous man in the window looking out, I realised I was that man. The artist hides himself in the painting. He is inside the painting, looking out.

T: If the artist hides himself in the painting, where are you hiding now that you are no longer painting?

There is nowhere to hide, least of all, talking to you. The unconscious is the only other hiding place I know.

T: As I said in the first session, the artist is like a child playing a game of hide and seek. It is a joy to be hidden but a disaster not to be found.

Perhaps it was a bit premature to suggest leaving our sessions.

T: Let us consider your capacity to repair your relationship with your mother and your father, to repair your relationship to yourself. What would it take for you to make these reparations?

*

One of Dad's paintings is on the cover of *The Vivisector*, a novel by Patrick White. The publisher gave him a copy. Dad passed it onto me. 'I can't read it. You might as well have it.'

I read David Marr's biography of Patrick White. I recognised my father—the talent, the dedication to the work, the desire for vindication of early negative reviews, the gap between one's sense of oneself and the exalted image others have of the writer, the artist, the relationship with failure, the shame, the cruelty to the supportive partner, the reclusiveness, the self-loathing. Patrick White is quoted as saying, 'My flawed self has only ever felt intensely alive in the fictions I create.'

He says to T:

It's a wonder I have not thought of this before. What if I do a portrait of you? It would present me with my greatest challenge, tackling the problem of a portrait of a person who is completely unknown to me. Maybe the struggle of this painting will allow me to repair myself, following your instructions.

T: Where would you start, with the head or with the feet?

I would start with what I know, the Persian carpet, more specifically the flaw in the Persian carpet. My flawed self is never more fully alive than in the paintings I create. What an opportunity. Two flawed selves sitting opposite each other.

I had painted a portrait of Tam Purves, the director of a gallery where I exhibited my work. He liked it so much he asked me to paint one of his wife, his co-director, who was very good at the business side of it. Artists feel somewhat beholden to the gallery directors who exhibit their work so I agreed to do it although I was not really keen to do so.

When Anne saw her finished portrait, her response was uncensored, undisguised. I believe that when she showed it to her mother, her mother burst into tears. 'You, of all people, should know that my portraits are not pretty,' I said. 'What did you expect? The Mona Lisa?'

A few months later I heard that the painting was included in an auction catalogue under the title *Woman in a Blue Suit*. 'The painting is a portrait,' I wrote back. My reputation was at stake. It was withdrawn from auction and I thought nothing more about it.

Some time later I learned that it had not been stored in one of the many places a painting could be stored by a couple who own an art gallery. It had been burnt in a little ceremony in their 44-gallon barrel drum in the backyard. They had attempted to conceal the sale at auction but they wanted me to know about the burning. They wanted to punish me. I could have told them the repercussions of burning a painting. The burning does not get rid of the offending item. It draws attention to the motivation for the need to destroy it.

T: You remembered the burning of a portrait just as you considered painting my portrait. If you painted my portrait, are you worried that I wouldn't like it, that I would burn it, that my mother would burst into tears?

I am worried that it would reveal too much of myself reflected back.

One day as I was leaving a visit to my parents, my father said pompously to my fourteen-year-old and twelve-year-old daughters, 'Cézanne said, "I have failed to realise my sensations." Life is a series of defeats.'

He says to T:

I am worried that I am too like my father. Working in the factory, my father was a defeated man. He did not keep his defeat to himself. He passed it onto me like a gambler passing on a wad of notes in an envelope under the table. By the time I realised what was in the envelope it was too late to return it. The artist's work is inherently one of defeat. The artist never lives up to his ambition.

When Lindsay told me that Pater had died, I put down the phone and poured myself a drink. It was not until I heard myself telling Helen that the reality of it struck me.

The next day I continued painting, not wanting to think about the significance, if indeed there was one.

Pater rarely took a day off work. He conscientiously took on his responsibility as the breadwinner. He lived within his means. We had the same temperament, keeping to ourselves, preferring the company of one or two others. It was from him that I took responsibility for being the breadwinner. I always had a job teaching although I would much rather have painted full time like artist friends.

Every now and then, after Mother died, it occurred to me that I should visit my father. I always found excuses—a painting to finish, an exhibition to prepare, a lecture to write. I knew that Lindsay had looked after our parents, helping them financially. I am ashamed to say that I allowed him to believe that my dedication to painting exempted me from keeping in touch with our parents. I never subscribed to the belief that an artist is granted a licence to ignore the rules that other human beings are obliged to follow.

T: You are appreciative of Lindsay and angry with your father.

When Mother protested about my decision to be an artist, Pater could have said, 'Let the lad do what he wants.'

The poet W.S. Merwin wrote a poem about the last time a man saw his father. The man didn't see his parents very often although they lived in the same city. The last time he saw his father, the father was asking about his life. The father tells the son he wants him to stay and talk to him. The father goes into the next room to get something to give his son but as he does so he notices the son looking at his watch. The father says that he doesn't want the son to feel like he has to stay if he has important work to do or someone to see, 'I don't want to keep you'. The son leaves but there is nothing he has to do and no one he has to see. That was the last time he saw his father.

I imagine that Dad's father may have been like the father in the poem, a father intimidated by his son, by his cleverness, by his status in the world.

He says to T:

It crossed my mind to see Pater after Mother died. I imagined my father would see me as a man who had made it in a way he had not made it himself. I felt that my presence would unnerve him. I didn't want to embarrass him. As I said, I felt atavistic guilt for making so much more money than my father.

On Helen's instructions I went to my father's funeral. 'You cannot not go to your father's funeral,' she said. She offered to come with me, but I said I would rather get the whole thing over and done with alone. In her absence she gave me instructions. 'You have to talk to people. You have to ask them who they are and how they know Mr Brack.' I asked a woman who she was. 'I'm your aunt.' After that I wasn't listening to Lindsay's eulogy. I was planning my escape.

T: This was an opportunity to think about what your father meant to you, to pay your respects. It was an opportunity to sit and listen to the eulogy. It wouldn't matter if you didn't talk to anybody.

I was obediently doing what Helen had told me to do.

I want him to find compassion for his father.

He says to T:

I never told Lindsay that I was grateful to him for looking after our parents, for helping them financially.

T: Unlike your brother, you carry the burden of remorse.

The next session he says to T:

This morning I stared at myself in the mirror, shaving. I saw my father's eyes, or what I remembered were his eyes. I realised I was the same age as my father when he died. I held the razor up to my cheek, put it down and then looked again in the mirror. A streak of blood marked the place where the razor had pierced me. The thought came to me: I am the same flesh and blood as my father.

In a novel by William Maxwell, the protagonist's mother dies in the flu epidemic of 1918. Many years later, after six months on the analyst's couch, he relives the night he paced with his arm around his father's waist, walking from room to room, stopping where his mother lay in her coffin. Together they stood looking at her. He meant to say to the analyst, 'I couldn't bear it,' but what came out of his mouth was, 'I can't bear it.' Then Maxwell writes, 'This statement was followed by a flood of tears such as I hadn't known before, not even in my childhood.' He gets up and goes out into the New York street, 'a place where one can weep on the sidewalk in perfect privacy.'

He tells T:

After the last session, I stepped outside onto the footpath, and as I did so, I remembered my father's words that day we returned from the country, 'It's nice to have the concrete under the feet.' Then I imagined, or thought I saw, a huge fissure open up in the concrete. I found myself uncontrollably sobbing in a flood of tears such as I had never known before, not even in my childhood.

Today I stopped in the place where the fissure had opened up like a chasm. I picked up one of the magnolia petals that were covering the pavement like a carpet. I examined the single petal as closely as I had examined my face looking in the mirror shaving. The petal was pure white on one side and wine-red on the other. I scooped up a handful, held them for a few moments and then let them fall in a little shower onto the concrete under my feet.

T: You are finding compassion for your father.

Silence.

T: If your heart can open for your father, could it also open for your mother? You do have the capacity to reconsider what you did in the past. You told me that you later regretted taking the position you did in *Collins Street 5pm*.

When I was first asked to give lectures on art, I remember telling the audience, 'My mother didn't want me to be an artist. She said it was just painting women with no clothes on.' I was ridiculing Mother for not knowing that the artist's model was referred to as 'the nude figure'. I knew I could get a laugh. Later I regretted it.

T: In mocking your mother for her ignorance you had demeaned yourself.

That's right. I can understand why Mother pushed us to do very well at school, why she wanted us to have jobs where we would earn a decent salary. My parents could understand what Lindsay did as an engineer but they saw no importance to the world in painting pictures. They weren't interested in something as frivolous or grandiose as 'the human condition'. They were concerned with how their sons could make enough money to live on. I don't blame them for that.

It is not only working-class parents who have ambitions for their sons. Near the beginning of Patrick White's novel *The Twyborn Affair*, the father, a judge, asks his son, '"What do you think of doing, Eddie?" You could hardly answer, Nothing; surely being is enough? looking, smelling, listening, touching. Instead you said, "I'm thinking of going into the country. To work."'

The father offers to get his son a job in a firm of solicitors with someone he knows. 'I'd die so much happier for seeing you dedicated to the Law.'

At the end of the novel Eddie has not entered the Law making his father happy. He is running a brothel and lives as a woman. 'He', now 'she', is sitting on a park bench when she sees someone coming towards her. It is her mother with whom she has had a torturous relationship. The women sit side by side until the mother rummages in her handbag, takes out a pencil and writes on the fly leaf of a prayer book. 'Are you my son Eddie?'

'No, but I am your daughter Eadith,' the other writes in response.

After a short pause, the mother says, 'I am so glad. I've always wanted a daughter.'

He says to T:

Mother wanted me to be a general in the army. My magnum opus was a painting of the Battle of Waterloo. I wasn't a general, but I had invested myself in a battle.

I want my father to reconcile with his mother. In a poem 'The Visitor', Mary Oliver writes how on a moonless night she hears a frantic knocking on the door. She knows it is her father who has returned from the dead to pay her a visit. For a long time she doesn't open the door but eventually the door opens of itself and she knows that she can bear what she previously found repellent in her father.

If Mary Oliver could do that, I could get my father to do that.

He tells T:

Some days in the early evening I heard a knocking on the door. For the first few days it was a wild furious knock, then a short sharp smack and then a gentle, persistent tapping. I knew who was knocking, but was not yet ready to open the door and face what I knew I must face.

After four days I got up from my chair and walked towards the door which opened by itself as I reached it. Mother was standing in the doorway. I was about to say, 'What do you want?' but I said nothing. I knew what she wanted.

We looked each other eye to eye. She had aged in the forty years since I had last seen her and yet she was indisputably my mother. She made a move to step over the threshold into the house. I offered no resistance. She sat down with the ease of one who had been here before while I continued standing, not quite knowing what to do with myself. I was aware of the point of contention between us: my paintings on the walls. As she focused her eyes on me, I heard myself saying, 'Would you like a cup of tea?'

'Yes, please, I'd love one,' she said. The sound of her voice took me back to my childhood when I was the 'one' that she loved. I left her alone while I went into the kitchen to make the cup of tea. A shudder of nervous anticipation rushed through me, but I could not allow it to get the better of me. It was years since I had made a cup of tea so I had to concentrate on the procedure. I put the kettle on the stove. I found the teapot Helen used. I found a crumpled box of tea leaves and put three spoons of tea into the pot. I gathered two cups and saucers and put them on a tray. I remembered to get the milk from the fridge. The thought came to me, 'Mother might like a biscuit.' I seemed to remember that she was partial to a biscuit with a cup of tea. I looked in the cupboard and found the biscuit tin Helen always used. I opened the tin. I did not recall having seen these biscuits before. They were not the sort Helen would eat and I never eat biscuits myself. One side of each biscuit was coated with pink or yellow icing and on the other side the raised image of a clock face. I wondered whether I should taste one to check if they were palatable, but as I am no connoisseur I placed them onto a saucer thinking that if Mother didn't like the look of them she didn't have to take one.

I brought the tea tray into the room where Mother was sitting but there was nowhere to put it. I placed it on the floor while I moved the book I was reading from the coffee table. I picked up the tray and placed it onto the table, aware of my clumsiness as Mother sat sedately. As I did this, Mother remarked, 'I see that you still like reading. You always had your nose in a book, I remember.'

'Yes, I still like reading,' I said, grateful for her small talk. I assumed she had glanced at my pictures on the walls while I was making the tea. If she had, she kept her thoughts to herself. I poured the tea, trying not to fumble, and as I handed her the cup, the thought came to me, 'This woman is my mother' as one might hold up one's hand and think, 'This is my hand,' fascinated that such a thing 'belonged' to oneself.

I poured myself some tea and offered the plate of biscuits. Mother took one with the pink icing, turned it over and said approvingly, 'Tic Tocs.' I realised she was announcing the name of the biscuit, the 'tic toc' referring to the clock face. She dunked the biscuit into the tea, holding it there for a few seconds, then took it out and raised it to her mouth and took a bite. I pictured the clock face dissolving in the hot tea as if time itself had dissolved between the present and the past. Mother's smile took me back to that memory of her praise and I found myself recalling what I saw and felt and knew when I was a little boy, awash with her loving attention to me.

In that moment, sitting in companionable silence with Mother, I remember feeling, 'This is marvellous,' as one thinks looking at a Rembrandt self-portrait for the first time. I picked up one of the Tic Tocs with the yellow icing, dunked it into the hot tea as Mother had done, held it there for a few seconds, put it into my mouth and swallowed it. My thawed self was never more fully alive than in that moment sitting with Mother after our long estrangement.

Mother said, 'I remember when Lindsay was a baby and you were two years old. My whole day was spent looking after you and Lindsay, doing the washing, the cooking, the ironing, the cleaning. I remember longing for the day when I would sit down and you would give me a cup of tea with a biscuit to nibble on.'

Mother had got what she longed for: the day when her first-born son would sit down and give her a cup of tea with a biscuit.

T: Sitting with your mother and having a cup of tea is one of your greatest achievements. Your mother got the cup of tea and a biscuit she had always wanted. What about you? Did you get what you always wanted?

Mother must have seen the paintings on the walls. In ignoring them she was saying she accepted me as I am. I did not need her to understand the paintings. I did not need her approval. This is what I felt was 'marvellous'. She had turned up. She had knocked on the door and she had accepted me for who I am.

*

In the next session he says to T:

I remember a teacher saying, 'You must make your mind a good companion because you live with it every minute of your life.' I had no friend. The teacher was telling me it was legitimate to make one's own mind a companion.

T: Have you done what the teacher advised? Have you made your mind a good companion?

It's certainly a better companion than it was. In fact, I think it is a good enough companion for us to end these sessions.

Last week, as I walked past the drycleaner's shop, I noticed several paintings of baby Jesus attached to the window. I stopped and looked. A sign said that they were painted by children from Grade 4B at St Mary's primary school. A nativity scene made of plasticine had been constructed by the children of 5A. Mary's head had fallen to the side and one of the donkeys had nearly collapsed as two of his legs could not support the weight of his plasticine body. I heard your words, 'There you are, finding fault, criticising other people's efforts.' At that moment I became aware of my reflection in the window: an old, dishevelled man. I became aware of another reflection looking in the window and my thoughts were interrupted by a woman's voice.

'My son Dominic painted some of that picture.'

Then I heard myself saying, 'So this must be his first exhibition. It's a lovely painting.'

T: You could find generosity within yourself.

As I told you, I have done what the teacher said. I have made my mind a good companion.

T: What are you going to do now?

I am going to do a painting of the window of a drycleaning shop. It will show the children's paintings of the three wise men attached to the window with a sign saying *By St Mary's Grade 4B and 5A*. It will show a plasticine nativity scene. In the background you will see a man standing near the rows of drycleaned coats and jackets in their plastic bags. The pièce de résistance will be my reflection outside the window, looking in. It will be my final self-portrait.

I once did a painting of a shop window of surgical equipment. Crutches dangled from a hook. At the bottom of the window, several walking sticks were displayed higgledy-piggledy with a sign saying, 'A walking stick makes a good companion.' The teacher said, 'We must make our mind a good companion.' If I had dementia, I would have no mind at all. I would have lost my mind. I would have no companion. You have been my walking stick, my good companion.

T: I have been your walking stick and now you have found the capacity to walk alone.

They are both silent for a while as if pretending to be listening to the rain.

T: Our time is up, all our time is up, this is the end of our work together.

Thank you. Thank you from the bottom of my heart.

They shake hands.

He walks out into the street and then enters a shop and buys an ice-cream. He sits on a seat near a playground watching the children playing. A ball lands near his feet. He picks it up and throws it back to the children and then he resumes eating the ice-cream.

Whether or not it is the grace of God, I like to think that it was grace that my father found when he sat on the seat eating the ice-cream, throwing the ball back to the children playing.

'Each of us has a public life and a private life. But beyond both is a secret life that baffles us.'

Richard Flanagan, *Question 7*

My Mother

My mother *had* found grace. She tells me how she was walking along a busy street when it started to rain. As she walked, she put one arm into the sleeve of her raincoat and was grappling with the other sleeve dangling behind her back when a hand appeared from behind, guiding her arm into the sleeve. The Guider-of-the-Arm continued walking, disappearing into the crowd, leaving my mother's thanks dangling with no one to receive them. 'Do you know what that was?' she said. 'That was the Grace of God.'

She does not see it as the kindness of strangers.

We were having lunch, our plates balanced on our knees. Our cups of tea perched precariously on papers covering a small coffee table. Nietzsche's *Being and Nothingness* peeped out from beneath a concert program partially covered by a bank statement, a glossy brochure for a gallery event jostled with the train timetable, a message to 'the householder', a postcard 'Dear Helen'. A single piece of paper in my mother's distinctive handwriting floated on the top. It read like the titles of her paintings.

The true but hidden self that is veiled by the flesh.
Everyday feelings of Guilt. The yearning for Redemption
for the blessing that relieves us of our Guilt.

My mother had not invited me to read what she had written but neither had she covered it up.

I wondered aloud about a man on trial for the deaths of an elderly couple whose bodies he burnt into smithereens. 'For the rest of his life he has to live with the guilt of what he did to their bodies,' I said. Understandably, my mother did not take my oblique reference to the guilt of another to speak about her own.

She had given other clues for what she was seeking. For a time, she would excitedly ask at family gatherings, 'Have you seen the television series *Queen Victoria*? There's a simply divine Lord Melbourne. We would all love a Lord Melbourne.' Curious to know her fascination with Lord Melbourne, I watched the television series.

At eighteen, Victoria becomes queen, consulting with the Prime Minister, Lord Melbourne, a man old enough to be her father. He advises her, coming when she calls him, guiding her, listening, endlessly patient, never ridiculing her for her ignorance about matters of the state. The beautiful young Queen Victoria falls in love with the charismatic Lord Melbourne who very properly does not surrender to either his or her desires. In my mother's hankering after her own Lord Melbourne, I saw her as yearning for a father who had the time to be there for her, guiding her, coming when she called him, listening to her worries.

When my mother was growing up, she did not see her father except to say good morning and good night. 'I told you, Dad left for work at seven-thirty in the morning and came home at seven at night.' The children were brought up by nannies. They had meals with Nanny in the nursery. On the weekends, their father saw his patients, went to his club and played golf. On holidays he drove them to a guesthouse where he left them in the care of Nanny.

For years I could not reach my father. On family occasions I asked him questions about art. Wanting something more but not knowing how to get it, I figured out that as he communicated to me in his paintings, I would respond to him in my form of painting. I devised a letter with photographs, binding it in the form of a book, telling him not to look at it until I had left to go home. Ten minutes after arriving home, the phone rang. It was Mum.

'John was so pleased with your book.'

A silence followed and then the clattering of her phone dropping and then: 'I wish my father had seen my paintings and understood them.'

In all the years of my mother's exhibition openings, I never saw her father or her mother. They would have received an invitation. She must have wondered why they weren't there.

I saw my father in his paintings. My mother did not see her father in his very private work, and in not coming to her exhibitions, he did not see her in hers. The title of a painting, painted in her nineties: *The desire to relate to a Superior Other but Not Seen by him.* A few years later: *There is no Feedback so is What I do Worthwhile? Self Doubt.*

As I saw it, my mother was giving clues about her deepest needs in her note left on the table, in her fascination with the television program, in the titles of her paintings. She was telling us her desire to be seen by a 'superior other', the desire for feedback on her work, for a father figure who had the time to show his love for her, who had seen her paintings and understood them, another human being who could offer redemption from her guilt.

The therapist had listened to my father. I was curious to know what would happen if a therapist listened to my mother. She would not actively seek out a therapist; she expressed her inner life in her paintings. She referred to 'that psychoanalytic stuff' as 'hopeless' as it applied to her painting and yet she read books by the psychoanalyst Adam Phillips. In a chapter 'On Not Getting It', she had written *too stupid* in the margins. She referred to those who did not 'get' her paintings as 'too stupid' to get them. In *Art as Therapy* she shouted into the margins: *YES!!! Not so!!!!! Art isn't about 'beauty'. Purpose of art? Self knowledge!?* She tells me she is reading a marvellous book on Hitler's childhood, hoping to discover why he did the evil things that he did.

It was not until after her death that she gave herself permission to tell the world her deepest troubles. In a fifteen-page speech to be read at her funeral, she revealed her thoughts about her painting, her relationship to Dad, her views on the art world, her private agonies and misgivings.

She knew from experience and humiliation that the seven deadly sins applied to her, to be navigated, and she knew from experience how distorting each deadly sin is when it dominates...She regretted her savagery to others, whilst condemning those who savaged her.

The speech to be read publicly at her funeral seemed more suited to the privacy of the consulting room of the therapist than the exposure of the public gathering of family, friends, artists and gallery directors. It read as a vindication to the art world, an appeal to be understood, an appeal to be absolved of her misgivings.

I had intended to create a scenario where my mother visits a therapist as my father had with T. At ninety-seven she would not consider seeing a therapist but I can imagine that she would respond to a stranger who would listen to her kindly. I will arrange for her to meet such a person. He will have the skills and experience of a chaplain, a doula, a spiritual advisor. He will have worked as a psychiatrist and in his retirement will have been called upon to hold the hands of those who are dying. His work as a psychiatrist will give him legitimacy in my mother's eyes. It will have given him the awareness of how we are shaped by our childhoods, the power of the unconscious, how we say one thing and mean another. He will have listened to stories of those who had never spoken of the child they were forced to give up for adoption, of those haunted by guilt of the crime they got away with, of those who had kept their sexuality hidden. He will offer not only what my mother experienced from the man who had helped her put her arm into the sleeve of her raincoat, but the opportunity to unburden herself of what troubles her and for which she is seeking atonement.

Given that she would not seek out the man I refer to as V, I will invent a scenario where he would find himself offering his companionship to her.

Mum sometimes received requests for information about her father as president of the Melbourne Club and his role in the formation of the Royal College of Psychiatrists. V will contact her to ask about her father as a member of the Melbourne Establishment. He will send a driver to collect her and bring her to his house not far from her childhood home. He will have the manners, the charm and the self-confidence of a man who was brought up with a sense of entitlement and who elicits respect from this entitlement. My mother will defer to this man who will remind her of her father. She will tell him of her grandfather Sir Henry Carr Maudsley who was knighted for his services in the First World War, and who was said to have occupied an exalted place in the history of Australian medicine. She will tell of her grandmother Lady Maudsley, daughter of Canon Stretch, who took a leading part in the social and artistic life of Melbourne. She will tell how, aged three, she had been ticked off by Lady Maudsley for slurping the butter out of a scone and how her grandfather had subsequently copied what she did, winking at her. She will tell of what she knows of her father's role in the First and Second World Wars and of his medical achievements.

Sessions with V

She says to V:

Dad was a darling man, so charming and conscientious, so hard-working. He didn't have it all easy. He was born with a cleft palate. The other boys at Melbourne Grammar teased him for his lisp. He figured out that to be accepted, he had to become very good at sport. And so he did. He trained very hard and won medals for his school. We hardly saw him, he was so busy at work. I remember when he called my sisters and me together. 'Look what I've got Mummy for her birthday.' He unwrapped a parcel. 'It's a lace tablecloth,' he said. 'Mummy will love it.'

The next day we eagerly watched as Mum unwrapped the birthday present he had bought. 'Take that back,' she said, tossing it aside. She had recognised the lace as the same lace as a doily that one of Dad's patients had made for him and given him not long after their first meeting.

V: It was then that you learnt that despite his considerable achievements, like all of us, your father had his flaws.

The reference to her father's flaws immediately summons up her own. She tells V what she told a family gathering in a speech on her ninetieth birthday.

It's all the things I did wrong that I remember. And then I think, I must have got something right, but perhaps I didn't.

V: You are asking for confirmation that you got 'something right'.

I am sure I did get something right. I am not a total and utter failure.

V: No, you definitely are not.

I really could have done better given my advantages.

V: You are very hard on yourself.

My work wasn't even mentioned in a major book on the history of Australian art. John's work was mentioned but nothing about mine. As if I didn't exist. Sometimes I wonder whether all my work will just go into the rubbish bin for all the interest that is shown.

V: It is very disappointing to you, very hurtful, to be excluded. At the end of your life, you are seeking some sign that your work has been worthwhile, that you yourself are worthwhile. Let us continue these conversations once a week.

Mum's work was not given the acclaim that was given to Dad's work. It is not as accessible, it is complex, not easily identifiable.

Unexpectedly, I once came upon a postcard of one of her early paintings in the gallery shop of the National Gallery of Victoria. It depicted a curved backbone with two white hexagon shapes at the top. A green wreath was clasped around the hips. Two lobster legs protruded, bent at the knees, their claw pincers dangling, supposedly the feet. In not preparing myself to see my mother's paintings as I did when I went to her exhibitions, I glimpsed how others might see them for the first time.

There was something disconcerting about the image, something almost repellent, cold and elusive. The image on the postcard was not pure abstract; neither was it purely realistic. The flesh had been drained from the body.

I turned the postcard over to read the title. *The Listening Lady*, 1956. A title leads us into the painting. This title confused me. What tells us the lady is listening? Despite the skill of the painting and the subtle beauty of the muted tones, I imagined that the postcards would be left there, discarded, as if saying, 'No one wants one of us.'

I found myself wishing to defend the painting against the criticism I myself was making. It was my mother's painting. I knew how hard she worked.

Something further unsettled me. On the back of the postcard next to the title I read, *Gift of the artist*. 'That's kind,' I thought, 'a gift.' I recalled Mum saying, 'I've given one of John's paintings to the gallery, the NGV. That's where his work will be most appreciated. I've included several paintings of my own.' For years, Mum was disappointed that the NGV had not bought one of her significant later works and rarely displayed the few early ones in its collection. She would rather the gallery bought a painting but since they had not, she had given several as a gift in a package they could not refuse. My admiration for her ingenuity in getting her painting into the gallery collection was overshadowed by the humiliation at the need to give such a gift.

A few days later, I came across a short item in the newspaper. '*Two Running Girls*, a John Brack oil on board, was sold at auction for $1.65m.' In 1959, when my father was painting *Two Running Girls*, my mother was cooking the meals for my father and the four of us girls. She was sewing and knitting most of the clothes and doing all the housework as well as doing her own painting and tending to the needs of the man who painted *Two Running Girls*.

His painting was sold for over one million dollars.

Her painting was given as a gift in a package of his paintings.

*

In the next session she says to V:

Every so often I wake up in the night with everyday feelings of guilt, yearning for the blessing that relieves us of our guilt.

V: Tell me about guilt.

Well, just everyday feelings of guilt. If I don't go for a walk, I feel guilt. If someone points out a mistake, I feel guilt. If I don't write the acceptance letter straight away, I feel guilt. Guilt about the murderous thoughts about John. Guilt about not being worthwhile. Guilt about my failings with the children.

V: Your guilt overwhelms you. You cannot let it go.

In noting the date of her marriage on my birth certificate and the date of my birth, I assume that she had to get married.

She tells V:

I remember the terrible guilt when I discovered that I was pregnant. I knew we would have to get married.

V: Instead of feeling joy that you were expecting a baby, giving your mother a grandchild, you were overcome with guilt.

Well, I hadn't planned to get pregnant. It was my fault. I also knew that I was disappointing Mum in not marrying some gorgeous young man, the son of a friend, a young man who was training to be a doctor, a lawyer, a diplomat. Here I was, marrying an artist from a family my parents had never even heard of. I was more determined than ever to prove that John could be successful as an artist, to prove that John was not a nobody.

*

In the next session she arrives with wet hair. She has walked from the car to V's room, not permitting the driver to accompany her with an umbrella.

V: Oh dear, I see you have been caught in the rain Helen. Would you like to lie down on the couch? Let me put a blanket over you.

I'm not an invalid, you know.

V: I know you are not an invalid. I just want to make you comfortable and warm. You can talk to me lying on the couch.

No no no. I would rather sit on the chair.

After a silence she says: As a child I *was* an invalid for one year. I was having fun with other children running and jumping from the sand dunes when I landed on a stick. It was excruciatingly painful. The pain of the walk from the sand dunes to the guesthouse where we were staying was like nothing I had ever experienced before. The stick had embedded itself into my foot so deeply you could not see any evidence of it. The foot felt terribly painful even after the stick was removed. No one believed me. How could the stick still be causing pain when it had been taken out? Later it was discovered that I had osteomyelitis caused by an infection from the stick.

V: That sounds traumatic.

Well, I don't know about 'traumatic'. I just remember the excruciating pain.

V: And initially no one believed you.

Often Mum feels that she is not believed, not heard, not understood. Dad did not believe her when she told him that Seurat was using the same technique they were being taught but when she showed him the book, 'he had to admit I was right'. She did a series of paintings on the theme of Cassandra after the mythical figure no one believed.

Mum had told V about the stick in her foot in their first meeting. There is another event in her life that I imagine she would tell someone who was prepared to listen.

She tells V:

About thirty years after my mother died, I got a phone call from a cousin I hardly knew. As we chatted about our childhoods, the cousin mentioned our common grandmother. I told her that she was mistaken, our grandmother had died before I was born. It seemed that the cousin had received letters and cards, Christmas and birthday presents, money for pony-riding lessons.

After I put down the phone, I looked up the Public Records Office where I discovered that Grace McCall died in Melbourne in 1946. At the time of her death, I was nineteen. The place of her death was not far from where I lived all my childhood.

V: Your parents had betrayed you.

It was the shock of it. I could not understand why our grandmother was kept hidden from the grandchildren who lived in the same city but not those who lived overseas. I wondered if she was mad or an alcoholic or had some horrible disfigurement.

I discovered that Grace McCall worked as a housekeeper for a Dr Laing. Dr Laing's daughter Nancy was a frequent visitor to our house. It could be that she was not just a housekeeper, she was living as the de facto wife of Dr Laing.

If it was known that Hal Maudsley's mother-in-law was living 'in sin', the reputation of the Maudsley family would have been damaged. As you know, Dad was president of the Melbourne Club and so was his father before that. They were very important members of the Melbourne Establishment, a close-knit group of doctors, lawyers, judges and politicians. If someone was in trouble with the law, a lawyer friend could oblige. If a daughter needed an abortion, illegal at the time, a medical friend could perform the operation. If the fees for the private school could not be paid, assistance was discreetly provided.

V: So, whatever the reason Grace McCall was hidden, it was beyond the expertise, the influence or the strings that could be pulled by the Melbourne Establishment.

It had to be kept from the Melbourne Establishment. A divorce, a driving offence or some other misdemeanour from a reputable family would be reported in the newspaper as a scandal.

Once, when sensing Mum's anger with her mother for keeping her grandmother a secret, I took the risk of asking her the question. 'How do you feel about your mother for keeping her own mother hidden?'

After a long silence she coldly replied, 'I never know what people mean when they ask me questions like that.'

She says to V:

There were other secrets to be kept in the family, things that were no one else's business. Dad was addicted to the morphine that he had for injuries in the war. It was a terrible, terrible ordeal for Mum getting him off the addiction. I remember all the whisperings and silence in those times of withdrawal.

V: You had to keep this a secret in the family.

Mum could get Dad off his addiction, but I could not get John off his.

V: Unlike your mother, you felt that you had failed.

I remember the doctor telling me that John's dementia was the result of his drinking. Nobody had told me he was an alcoholic. That beautiful brain going down the gurgler. If I had known John was an alcoholic, I would have done something to prevent it. I *did* do something. More than once, I poured the bottle of whiskey down the sink, thinking it may as well go down the plughole as into John's stomach.

V: Perhaps you knew there was nothing you could do to stop John's drinking.

I should have known that he was drinking too much. I should have known that his drinking would cause brain damage. It was stupid of me not to know. I remember being struck by the lovely German woman who managed the guesthouse where I was staying in Berlin. She said to me the first morning at breakfast, 'You know, we had no idea what was going on during the war. We knew nothing about it. We were as shocked as anyone when we found out.'

V: You are telling me that we can know something but also keep it a secret from ourselves.

I remember hearing cries like a wild animal in the night. It was terrifying. I didn't know what it was until Mum told me it was Dad calling out in dreams. In the First World War he was straight out of medical school, a medical officer in the Field Ambulance, the first on the scene after battle. Nothing in his medical training could have prepared him for what he experienced in the war. He did not talk about it although there were little glimpses in the diaries he had written.

V: Publicly your father was applauded for his bravery in the war. Privately he suffered the trauma of the war.

As a psychiatrist he gave shock treatment to those who had suffered what was known as shellshock. I understand it was very effective.

The psychoanalyst Nicolas Abraham refers to the 'dead who...took unspeakable secrets to the grave'. While the secret itself goes to the grave, the knowledge of a secret 'haunts' the living. The 'concealment of some part of a loved one's life' produces 'a gap' in the children and grandchildren. 'What haunts are not the dead, but the gaps left within us by the secrets of others.'

For years Mum made repeated references to the 'feral', speaking with revulsion of what humans do to each other. I assumed her reference to the feral arose from her disgust with the feral within her. Now I wonder whether it refers to the haunting of her father and her grandfather. Many of her paintings depict the symbols of war, floating shards, disembodied remnants, fragments. The titles of the paintings:

> *Our Civilised Minds, Our Feral Mindlessness, Our Inherited Language; our Re-configuration. The Hyena Laugh,* 2013.
>
> *Not 'The Civilized and the Barbaric'. But, 'The Civilized and the Feral'*, 2013.

Perhaps the haunting passed on from her father and her grandfather found expression in the images and the titles of the paintings.

In response to Mum's comments about the trauma of her father in the First World War, V says: Your father took unspeakable secrets to the grave. You are haunted by what you do not know of those secrets. You are experiencing what we now refer to as 'intergenerational trauma', the trauma passed on from one generation to the next.

I don't know. That just sounds like poppycock to me.

I do not know my mother's experience of the haunting. The stoicism of her class and generation meant that one battled on with little sympathy for those who drew attention to a discomfort, let alone a trauma they could not explain. The titles of two paintings, twenty years apart:

Not Safe to Reveal, Held in the Darkness, 2004.

Knowingly Hidden; Covered, Not Seen Not Revealed, 2024.

I do not know the secrets my mother carried from her childhood, but I *do* know her response to me telling her a secret from my childhood.

I was ten years old, walking home after playing at a friend's house after school. A man approached me. He told me he was lost. He asked me where [name of street] was. I cannot explain what led me to follow the man. I had been put under a spell. He spoke to me kindly. I was obediently doing what he asked of me.

When we reached the creek, I lay down by the creek bed as the man asked. I had no will. The man did what I later understood was rape. I cannot remember any pain. I cannot remember fear. I was looking down from above, observing myself.

For months I lay in bed at night imagining the headmaster calling me to the front of the whole school on Monday morning assembly, pointing to me, saying 'This girl is pregnant.' I did not know what had prompted this fantasy as no child had ever been called up and ridiculed in front of the school. I know now that this was the shame of the rape.

The shame was compounded by the guilt that I should tell my mother. I could not imagine telling her. It would be my fault. She would ask me why I had disobeyed her, talking to a stranger. She had enough worries looking after my father and three younger children. I had no language to describe what the man had done to me. As a ten-year-old I could spell 'camouflage' and 'deciduous trees' but I had never come across the words 'vagina', 'penis' or 'rape'.

In my early thirties I wrote a letter telling my mother what had happened at the creek bed. I wanted her to know. The burden of the secret was now exacerbated by the burden of the writing, which I hoped would release me from the secret. After so long in hiding I could not burst out spontaneously describing what had happened. I had to consider how to tell my mother, how to prepare her for what no mother would want to hear.

After more than six months I dropped the letter into the letterbox. Three days later I opened the front door to see my mother holding a plant wrapped in cellophane and done up with a ribbon. 'It's a...' she said, naming the plant. 'I bought it from a nursery on the way here. It likes shade.'

I took this gift on the unexpected visit as my mother's way of saying she had read the letter. I invited her in and put the kettle on the stove.

'I wonder if that happened to Vicky. One day she came home from school covered in bruises.' Mum wondered aloud about Vicky until I had composed myself sufficiently to suggest going outside to plant the shrub she had bought. My two young daughters assisted with the planting, innocent of the meaning of it. My mother had not responded as I feared she would if I had told her when it happened. She did not imply that it was my fault. It would not be characteristic of her to warmly give me a hug and say, 'I'm so sorry.' It surprised me that I was not more upset by her reaction and yet it confirmed why I had not told her when it happened.

In not telling my mother before then, I had wanted to protect her. She had so many worries. One more worry could undo her. As the eldest child, I knew that it was up to me to help look after the younger children, to make things easier for Mum, not to be any 'trouble', not to make any additional demands on her. If she fell apart, who would look after us? Who would look after Daddy?

Mum tells me, 'You were about two years old. I was sewing. You were playing. It was raining. Suddenly there was a crash of thunder and then lightning, and then I looked up to see you running into the room holding the baby, the baby's head narrowly missing the doorway.'

I do not remember carrying the baby, but I do remember slipping the holiday pocket money from my grandmother into my mother's purse.

At the time I posted the letter about the rape, I did not have to protect my mother anymore. My responsibilities were to my children. I was free of the secret, but I had given my mother the burden of knowing of the rape. As far as I know, there was no one she could talk to about it.

Twenty years after sending the letter, the proceedings of the royal commission into institutional responses to child sexual abuse were reported in the newspapers. I asked Mum if she had been following the news.

'Yes, I have. It's terrible. It's truly terrible what happened to those children. I cannot bear thinking about it.'

'Yes, it's awful,' I said. 'Imagine being sexually abused by someone in authority, someone you trusted, someone your parents trusted, a teacher, a Catholic priest.'

'It's too awful to think about,' my mother said.

'It takes courage to tell what happened, especially publicly in a royal commission.'

'Yes,' my mother agreed, and then, looking vacantly into the distance as if not speaking to me, she said, 'Some people can't even tell their mothers, you know.'

'Yes, I *do* know,' I replied.

My mother was telling *me* that *some people* could not tell *their* mothers.

'It's not just the abuse that's so damaging,' I said. 'It's the secrecy of it, the years of keeping the secret.'

On the way home I wondered if Mum remembered the letter. After the visit with the plant, the rape had never been referred to again.

A few weeks later, we were talking about the funny things little children say. Mum said, 'John was walking over the bridge at the creek at the bottom of the hill. A little girl ran up to him saying, "Are you a stranger?"'

It was uncanny. That was the bridge I saw from my vantage point lying face down on the creek bed as the man raped me.

After telling my therapist about the rape, I realised that I needed someone to tell me it was a violation. I needed someone to tell me that it wasn't my fault.

I do not know what secrets my mother is carrying but I want her to have the release from the burden of keeping the secret, despite not knowing what the secret is or indeed whether there is one.

How would I get my mother to tell V the secret she is carrying?

At age eleven she was in bed for one year with osteomyelitis, in the care of a nurse in a huge Victorian mansion. An odd-job man would be chopping wood, a housekeeper mopping the floors, tradesmen delivering things to the house. I picture the young girl wheeled out into the garden on a chaise longue, left there with her drawing pad and pencils while the nurse returned to chores inside the house. I picture a gardener chatting to the young girl who could not walk, confined to her chaise longue. I picture him bringing flowers for her to draw, tearing one apart, his calloused hands tenderly gripping the stamens and the petals, explaining the parts of the flower to her. I resist writing the hand reaching under the woollen tartan blanket, its tassels dangling onto the grass. Vaguely I picture the chaise longue capsizing with the body of the big man on top of the girl, one hand over her mouth suppressing her scream, the pages of the sketches of the parts of the flower loosened from the drawing pad, fluttering on the newly manicured lawn.

I wondered what stopped me from the description of the act of violation.

Perhaps I did not want to imagine that this had 'happened' to my mother. Perhaps it was because I heard her saying, 'No, that didn't happen.' Perhaps it was because I could not imagine my mother telling another person. Perhaps my desire for my mother to tell the secret arose from my wish to be free of the haunting of what I did not know and what I would never know.

I was disappointed not to have breathed life into this fictional scenario. I had wanted my mother to be free of the shame of the secret, to be free of the burden of keeping a secret.

It was not only that. I wanted something from V. I wanted to create a scenario where he would lovingly embrace my mother and say, 'I am so, so sorry.'

*

She says to V:

Mum was an enormous support for Dad. She didn't put up with any nonsense. I once heard a colleague of Dad's describe her as 'somewhat terrifying', adding that she had 'a wonderfully kind heart'. She was an amazingly competent woman. She could have been a matron in a hospital. Her job was managing the household, doing volunteer work and social activities required of Dad's work. That's what doctors' wives did in those days. She had a strong sense of noblesse oblige. She was president of the Truby King League of Victoria; she did a lot of work for Travellers' Aid. I didn't really see much of her except on Sunday afternoon and Nanny's day off.

V: So who looked after you in the absence of your mother?

We were looked after by nannies. I had become very fond of Nanny Stevens. One day she wasn't there. Replaced by another nanny. I didn't understand it. No one told me why she wasn't there and wasn't coming back. Later I wondered if she had left to get married. I waited for her to come but she never did.

V: The person you loved was taken away from you without any explanation.

I thought it must have been my fault. I wondered if I had said something to upset her.

V: There was no one to console you.

Well, you know, you just get on with life. What else is there to do?

V: I am wondering if you can feel for that little girl whose nanny she loved was taken away from her. I am wondering if you could consider the loss and bewilderment for that little girl.

She winces at what she would see as sentimentality and then says: It was a long time in the past. You get over it.

V: It is difficult for you to hear what must have been painful for you as a child. I am wondering if you could be sympathetic to your own wounded younger self.

That's just pathetic. I told you, you just get over it. That's just rubbish.

Mum was not given to expressions of sympathy or grief either for herself or for others. It appalled her that her mother had 'wailed for a week' after the dog died. 'I mean, all about a dog. It's pathetic.' We were discussing a book we had both read, the story of a woman who tamed a hawk as a way of working through her grief after the death of her father. 'I don't know why she had to go on and on about the father. A grown-up woman going on about how she misses him. It's so tedious. Why couldn't she just get over it? I mean, I ask you. It's just too silly for words.' She asked about my daughter who had postnatal depression. 'She's much better,' I said. 'Oh good, I am glad she's recovered.' I was giving the answer she wanted to hear. Her question 'How are you?' was often followed with, 'If you're not all right, don't tell me. I don't want to know.'

After V invites her to be sympathetic to her own wounded younger self, she doesn't turn up to the next session. She doesn't let V know that she won't be coming.

When she returns, she says to V: Oh, so you are here?

V: You thought I might have given up on you, abandoned you like Nanny Stevens.

No no no. I imagined that you were sitting looking out the window wondering where I was.

*

At Mum's ninetieth birthday we had gathered for afternoon tea—four children, ten grandchildren, two great-grandchildren and Mum's cousin Edward and his wife. At one point in the proceedings Mum said she wanted to read a speech. Later she gave me a copy.

'It is fun to be ninety, more fun than eighty-nine.'

This seemed disingenuous. Mum considered 'fun' to be superficial.

'Now for regrets. I regret that you have all done more for me than I have for you. I regret that I wasn't kinder to people. I must have got something right but maybe I didn't.' She concluded by saying how proud she was of us all. The pride in us all felt as disingenuous as 'it is fun to be ninety'.

After half-hearted applause a silence followed. I knew what I was expected to say but no words would come. No words would come from anybody else until Edward, perhaps sensing that something needed to be said, remarked on the wonderful spread of cakes that had been provided. This reminded Mum of a memory from her childhood.

'I was three years old. It was Easter. We had gone to visit Grandmother and Grandfather. I picked up a scone and slurped the butter out of the middle. Grandmother looked at me scowling, "Don't do that." Grandfather picked up a scone and copied what I did, winking at me.'

That's what she wanted, someone to wink at her, to acknowledge her, someone to say she had been a good mother, to say that she had got something 'right'.

In her vulnerability she says to V:

You have to remember that our family was based on the manners of the British upper class. Mum loved the Queen. When the Queen visited Melbourne in 1954 Mum went to great lengths to get us an invitation to the garden party. John would have hated it. Mum just assumed we would take up the invitation, furious when we didn't.

V: You had very different values from your mother and yet you carry the manners she instilled.

I was prohibited from eating any of the scrumptious-looking cakes at the ninetieth birthday as two days after I was scheduled for a bowel cancer operation. I told my friend Frances about my despondency at having failed my mother in not responding to her speech. She made a cup of tea and offered me a piece of orange cake she had made. As my eyes met the cake, I visualised the page of rules to follow before the operation. 'No food' and before that 'only white food, white rice, white chicken, white bread'. This was orange cake.

My hand reached out and picked up what was forbidden. I took one bite and then another. It felt like an act of defiance against my mother. 'No means no.' It was not only that. We had been sharing our feelings about our respective family gatherings. A piece of cake is the epitome of sharing.

Mum would reject the offer of 'sharing'. I could not think of a friend she could ring to tell of her disappointment at the response to her ninetieth birthday speech. She tried so hard to do or say the right thing without questioning the wisdom of what she perceived as the right thing. How could you be wrong if you were so conscientious? Before giving a talk or opening an exhibition she would spend hours studying the paintings, taking notes, writing and revising her speech with a diligence that often seemed out of proportion to what was being asked of her. I remember once walking her back to her car when her thoughts spoke themselves aloud, 'All that effort, but for what?' Despite the applause, the thanks, the bouquet of flowers, something was missing. As she says in her funeral speech: 'If I had known what was right, I would have done it.'

Perhaps if she had known love from her mother, if she had known the love of her grandmother, she would not have punished herself for what she saw as her failings. I have no doubt that her mother and father did love her, but they were not there for her. She berates herself, seeking affirmation that she did get something right but even if we reassured her—'You were a good enough mother'—I doubt those words would have consoled her. Who were we? We were 'only' her children.

*

She tells V:

From the age of five I was taught at home by a governess. I was very conscientious. When I turned eight, I started at St Catherine's. Instead of being in a class of three others, I was in a class of twenty others. I hated it. In some lessons I was far ahead, seen as a know-all, and in other lessons I was way behind, seen as a dunce. It was awful. I could never figure out what the teacher expected from me. If I had known what was right, I would have done it. At home I was expected to do well at my schoolwork, but I was also expected to be socially acceptable which meant not being serious about my work. When I got older, I was expected to be glamorous but not too glamorous, clever but not too clever.

V: You had a lot to be bewildered about. Your nanny left with no explanation. You were thrust into a class of twenty other children, in some subjects way ahead, in others way behind. You were expected to do well at school but not too well. It is understandable that you would be wary of trusting authority.

Long silence.

Twice in my life I did trust authority.

V: Tell me about it.

After I left the gallery school, I was very unsettled. I didn't know what sort of artist I wanted to be. I knew that I *didn't* want to do realistic painting, but I didn't know what sort of painting I *did* want to do. Then, by chance, I discovered the direction I would take.

Every day I sat opposite the same woman on the tram. I had never seen anyone like her before. I couldn't say what fascinated me. I wanted to draw her portrait, but I knew I could not sit opposite her sketching from the model as we were trained to do at art school.

When I got home, I drew a sketch of her from memory, playing with the image, stylising it, exaggerating shapes, moving bits around. Eventually I'd got it. The drawing looked like her, but it was not like a portrait. It wasn't like any other drawing I had ever seen. I didn't know if it was rubbish. I showed it to a respected art critic who said, 'That is the most erotic drawing I have ever seen.' It was one of the most encouraging things anyone had ever said to me about my work. I was young and naïve. At nineteen I had never heard the word 'erotic'. It was the 'erotic' that had fascinated me. It was the erotic that the drawing depicted. For me this was my *Opus 1*.

V: The respected art critic gave you permission to continue this approach to drawing.

He had shown me the direction to take. I had stylised the woman with exaggerated shapes. Over the years the subjects became more and more stylised and pared back. Numbers, letters and disembodied objects float across the canvas: a pillar, a crown, a doorknob, a shoe. The paintings play with perspective. Depending on how you look at it, a ladder is going up or down, the window is looking out or looking in. The Mobius strip, a three-dimensional figure eight, twirls back into itself, making the inside become the outside.

The titles were originally short—*The Journey, The Encounter, The Listening Lady*. But then, another man I respected suggested longer titles. He suggested writing in the title what I had told him about the painting. From then on, I wrote longer titles and then even longer. When they became even longer I called the paintings 'visual essays'.

V: Your work has been very much in response to the advice of these two men you respected. Their suggestions gave it legitimacy.

*

In 2017, an exhibition of Mum's work was held at the National Gallery of Victoria with three other women artists. The critic Sasha Grishin wrote that since first encountering her work, he was struck by 'its complexity, its quiet, reserved beauty and the intellectual engagement'. As he says, 'The paintings do not leap off the walls crying for attention, but once you pause for a moment, look and enter the work, you are drawn into a visual and intellectual labyrinth of endless complexity.' He concludes by saying, 'Maudsley is not a difficult artist to appreciate, but there is a certain threshold to overcome before you can enter her intriguing and perplexing world.'

Standing at the threshold, some ask, 'What's the code?' Infuriated at being asked, Mum made this into the title of a painting, thereby showing us the origin of the titles.

She tells V:

As I said, the titles come from what I am thinking at the time of doing the painting. It infuriated me when people asked for the code—as if there *was* a code—so I made that the title of the painting.

'I Want to be In It'; 'There's Nothing to be In On' 'What's the Code'

'There is no Code' 'This is Rubbish and you're not Getting Away with It'

V: The title is a retaliation to those who didn't get their meaning.

They were too stupid to get it. Once my work had finally become better known, I got the impression that young women artists thought I knew things I didn't. They thought I had a special trick of getting my work into a gallery, of having articles written about my work. They saw that I had got something they wanted, and they were determined to get it. When I told them that was rubbish, I couldn't tell them how to get it, they didn't want to know me. It's not as if your work is accepted just by magic. It's not as if you can tell someone in a sentence, passing it on so they can do it themselves. So then I made that the title of the painting.

> *'You Know Something that I don't, and I Want it; I'm the same as You'*
>
> *'No you're Not. I haven't Got what you think I've Got.'*
>
> *'Yes You Have and you wont let me Have it, but if I Match you, I'll Get it.'*
>
> *'When you find out I Haven't Got what you think I've Got. I will be your Enemy.'*
>
> *'If I don't Get it and Everyone else Does, I'll look Stupid, so I Pretend to*
>
> *Get it, but I'll Hate you. When No one Gets it, I'll join the Pack and Kill you. If*
>
> *you withstand this, You're Mad'*

V: So that is the title of one painting?

As I said, they are visual essays.

V: The titles of the paintings are doing something with your anger.

When my work was not included in a book on the history of Australian art, I painted several pictures, *The Power of The Written Word. Without the Written Word, Art doesn't Exist.*

V: The title reads as an invitation to write about your work.

She says nothing.

In the next session V asks:

I am wondering how the words of the title connect to the visual image of the painting.

Well, sometimes there are motifs in the picture connecting to the title—question marks, symbols, letters of the alphabet.

V: So the motifs or symbols are there to be deciphered in reference to the words of the title.

Well, you know the title means what it says because I say it. It's like the mother saying to the child, 'No means no.'

When Emily was little, sometimes I was asked to keep an eye on her to see that she didn't get into mischief. It was then that I discovered that two-year-old Emily had a will of her own and was not the extension of a doll. I have never forgotten it. I could not get her to obey me. It infuriated me. No means no.

V: It infuriates you when people do not get the titles.

I just don't understand it.

For Mum 'no means no', except when no means yes. She once said not to come to her exhibition opening, 'Too much trouble to get there.' Later I discovered she was disappointed I wasn't there.

Once, she was giving a talk when a man came in late and sat down, 'Come in darling man,' she said, welcoming him in with a gesture of her arm.

'Who is darling man?' I asked her later.

'Who?'

'The man who came in late.'

'Oh him. Isn't he revolting. He insists on carrying my bags to the car.'

*

She says to V:

As I told you, I was brought up in a family where manners were important. A child would stand up when a grown-up came into the room. We were gracious, polite and deferential to adults. You wouldn't say that you didn't like the meal. You would say it was delicious. In conversation the woman asked the man about himself. You wouldn't expect him to ask about you. You kept your real thoughts to yourself. The titles of my paintings are not like manners. They are my real thoughts.

V: A diary of the real thoughts of an artist.

Exactly. The titles are asking, 'How do we get permission for our innermost selves?' In fact, that is the title of a painting.

Mum was brought up in a family where one kept one's true thoughts to oneself. She was brought up in a family of secrecy—the secrecy of the grandmother she never knew, the secrecy of her father's addiction to morphine, the secrecy of her father's trauma from the war. I do not know how the impulse to secrecy is transmitted from one generation to the next, but I do know that I inherited my mother's propensity for secrecy without being aware that I had. It amazed me that someone could come into a room and report on an incident on the way there, that they could name the feeling of shock, right at that moment, drawing attention to themselves. One kept one's feelings to oneself, deferring to others.

The conditions of an artist's work enter the work. An artist in a small studio will be restricted to painting small works. An artist with only charcoal to work with will be limited by the materials available. The psychological conditions also enter the work. Those who are accustomed to secrecy may not even realise that they are withholding some little detail, some fact that would make sense of the work. Reflecting on my own process of writing gives me some insight into an explanation for my mother's process of painting.

This is my experience. You write something and then, thinking that you might have revealed too much, you hide some of it, leaving the vestige of what you wanted to say. You anticipate the guillotine striking you down: 'You can't say that. That is forbidden.' You do not even think to say what is obvious, even something the reader needs to know to make sense of what you have written. You want the reader to know without telling them. You assume that something deeply felt is libellous or incriminating. You hide it before knowing you have hidden it. You are withholding without knowing you are withholding. You strive to make sense with the fragments you permit yourself to write. It is painstaking, time-consuming. You think you are crafting a piece of writing when in fact you are ingeniously concealing something that cannot be said. You feel a constant frustration between the desire to say something and the impulse to conceal.

I noticed that other writers were not so constrained. I was envious of their eloquence, wondering how they did it. I thought it was talent or something to do with writing. I did not realise I was inhibited by this self-imposed rule until I became receptive to the inner voice asking why I was making it so difficult. But then, having recognised what I was doing, I did not release myself from the straitjacket, flinging it off in the liberation of release. It was an effort to remove it. It had become attached. I looked for guides from other writers to give me permission to write—women writers who had returned from the silence of the deep. The freedom of release was shadowed by mourning, mourning the years of having inhibited myself.

It was suggested that this was a form of sabotage. As I understand it, 'sabotage' would involve taking the scissors to the work, savagely cutting it into pieces, leaving a trail of blood in its wake. This sabotage is creative. It involves a huge amount of laborious work, saying something and then retracting most of it, concealing what might be too private.

I recognise the sabotage in my mother's work. An ornate letter 'A' floats across the painting called *Know Thyself*. 'What is the letter A?' I ask my mother.

'Can't you see? It's the self.'

I wonder if A is for artist, the self that writes the letter A. It is not obvious to me. It is to my mother. I assume that, like me, she is leaving too much space between the dots for the reader to join up. She knows how the motifs floating across the canvas connect to the titles but is mystified that others cannot make out the connection.

She says to V:

My paintings are not for the ordinary viewer but I could never understand why they were not understood by the art world. I didn't understand what I was doing wrong.

I had applied for a grant for a painting to be made into a tapestry. My work was ideally suited to this medium with its straight lines and clearly delineated patches of colour. A tapestry had already been made of my work. I wrote the application, draft after draft explaining my ideas about transposing a painting into a tapestry. Various of the children offered to type up the application but I said that my handwriting was perfectly acceptable and when they pointed out something called 'the selection criteria' I told them I wasn't going to answer that incomprehensible rubbish. I didn't understand it. I wasn't even on the shortlist.

V: Perhaps you were sabotaging your work or perhaps you felt entitled to receive the grant despite not following the application guidelines.

I don't know. That ridiculous form to fill in, that stupid woman whose work had been chosen. And then there was that woman who had befriended me, asking me for help. She was very polite and gracious but she was doing these simplistic landscapes out of some sort of fabric and weaving and pearls. Very decorative but not really serious. She had approached an art gallery in Berlin to exhibit her work. I wouldn't dream of doing such a thing. My work was far more serious than hers. I had given her advice and there she was getting an exhibition in Berlin with these decorative things she was making.

V: She dared to do what you would not permit yourself.

And Emily, my sister. Twelve years she took to finish her university degree which should have taken six years. Dad paid for her to stay in the university college, paying the fees every year she failed. I wouldn't dream of failing. And then there was John's friend Elizabeth Summons, just a fundraiser for the gallery school, one of those society ladies who dresses up for lunch. Not a serious person. John was enchanted with her, flattered that she bought a painting when not many other people did. A week after John died she gave me a rose bush called 'first love' with a card saying, 'In memory of John'. I mean, I ask you.

V: You are struggling with your envy.

No no, it wasn't envy.

In her funeral speech Mum tells us that 'she knew from experience and humiliation that the seven deadly sins applied to her' but when V names the sin of envy she denies it. In wondering about her capacity for insight into herself, I recalled the burning of Dad's portrait of Anne Purves. 'I don't know why Anne had to say that she burnt the portrait. She should have said she'd loaned it and then it disappeared. If she had said that, John would have kept exhibiting at the gallery, bringing in commissions from the sales.'

It surprised me that Mum did not see the burning as punishment to Dad for a portrait the sitter didn't like. She was not a stranger to the pleasures of punishment as revenge. On letting her know that we were not extensions of a doll, the four of us daughters had received pages and pages of letters, the pen running away with her, one vitriolic insult after another. Her punishment was not often spoken directly where it would elicit a response. It was written in the title of a painting, a letter, a report to someone else. I hear her saying, 'This idiot man V thinks he knows all about me but he doesn't. All this rubbish he goes on with.'

*

For the next week V has let her know that he won't be there. She forgets and waits for thirty minutes. In the next session she says:

You weren't here last week.

V: I am sorry, I did remind you.

Well, you weren't here.

V: You are angry with me.

No, I'm not angry. Sometimes I just wonder whether anybody cares. I barely sold enough paintings to cover the cost of the exhibition. I wonder if anything I do is worthwhile. All my paintings may as well go into the rubbish bin for all that anybody cares.

My mother despairs that for all the attention her work has received, it 'may as well go into the rubbish bin', and yet she ensures that it will be lasting, using proper paints, proper canvases, varnishing and frames. I tell her that Van Gogh did not get worthy recognition until after his death and neither did any number of women artists whose work remains undiscovered. It does not reassure her.

She tells V:

I really should have done better, considering my advantages. I mean, Dad was a very substantial person. A very serious person, very respected in the medical world. He had a name, a reputation. All I've done is paint pictures which only a few people buy.

V: You are comparing yourself unfairly with your father. He was not raising four children. He was not doing the work of supporting a husband. He was a doctor, you were an artist; very different offers to the world.

As I said, Dad was a very substantial person.

V: What would it take to see yourself as a substantial person, to see your considerable achievements, to see yourself as worthwhile?

It's all just poppycock to me. I don't understand this airy-fairy nonsense. It's just a waste of time. I could be painting. I don't even know why I'm here.

She doesn't turn up to the next two sessions and doesn't ring to say she isn't coming.

In the next session she says to V:

I thought you might not be here.

V: You were punishing me. You were punishing me for inviting you to see your own goodness, your own achievements.

She says nothing.

V: You could hear the respected critic who said, 'That is the most erotic drawing I have ever seen.' You could hear advice from the man who suggested longer titles; and yet, you find it difficult to hear advice suggesting that you have greater respect for your own work, that you see your work as significant, that you see yourself as significant.

I don't know.

After a long silence she says: You are not my father.

V: Perhaps you are punishing me for not being your father.

As she gets up to leave, he notices that she is quietly weeping. He puts his arm gently around her shoulder and says, 'I will see you at our next session.'

*

Mum's paintings were inextricably a part of the house. She got up on the ladder and painted the walls the same grey, purple, olive-green, blue as her paintings. Objects in the house appeared in the paintings: a doorknob, the back of a chair, a shoe. I recognised the 'withdrawal' of the titles as Dad's withdrawal with depression. When Dad had dementia, a painting was named *The Inhabitant Has Gone*.

One Sunday afternoon not long after Dad died, I visited Mum with the grandchildren. We brought her a CD player. With no horizontal surface free of household objects, I set up the ironing board and it was from there that we heard the voice of Joan Sutherland singing *Lucia di Lammermoor*. As the late afternoon approached darkness, Mum gave no sign of wanting us to leave and as the time stretched on, I felt the anticipation that something ominous would happen. Then I remembered that Dad had died. He would not be coming in from the studio asking me why I was still there and why Mum was not getting the dinner.

After Dad's death Mum was free of his demands. She had the house to herself without Dad's grumblings about the décor she selected. Sometimes journalists came to the house to interview Mum about Dad's work or her own. After the first of these interviews, I asked Mum how it went. 'I'm not into that Heide rubbish,' she said, referring to the stories of the private lives of the artists and benefactors who gathered at a place known as Heide. '"Private is private, public is public," I told the journalist.' She was warning *me* not to say anything about the private life of our family.

In marrying Dad, Mum had defied her family but in advocating 'private is private', she was continuing her family's rule of protecting the reputation of the important man. Until the journalist had come to the house, there was no need to articulate the rule. It occurred to me that we think we are escaping what we wish to escape from our childhood but we carry with us what has imprisoned us.

When journalists visiting the house wrote up an interview, they might respectfully refer to the 'cosily cluttered home'. I had lived in that 'cosily cluttered' home, or rather an earlier incarnation of it. I knew where to find the cups and saucers. I knew the location of the secret drawer where Mum's jewellery was hidden.

My description starts with the front door which opens into an open-plan sitting room. Mum's chair faces the television. Almost every horizontal surface is covered with an accumulation of books, newspapers, knitting, coats, concert programs, vases of dried lavender, the current TV guide. A Chinese bowl from an ancient dynasty sits on the sideboard alongside a pair of nail scissors and bandaids spilling out from the box. Walking down a short passageway, we enter the kitchen–living room.

The kitchen benches are covered with a collection of jars, bottles, bowls, packets of tea, raisin bread, a basket bursting with plastic bags. The only blank space is a chopping board on which is placed a sharp knife and the powdery remnants of a pill chopped into quarters. A long dining-room table holds a collection of vases containing wilting or dried flowers, often including a once-magnificent bouquet, a gift for opening an exhibition. Cobwebs hold the petals of dried-up roses together; petals fall onto the table. A recently picked rose or daphne might be placed in a glass vase near the end of the table, visible from my mother's armchair, a designer chair covered in a cabbage-green suede-velvety fabric.

The little coffee table cluttered with books and papers sits between the two designer chairs, one for Mum and the other for the visitor to sit having lunch.

Through an open door one glimpses into what is known as 'the painting room'. This is where Mum works on her painting. The floor is barely visible. It is covered with layers of drawing and tracing paper marked with geometric pencil lines. A narrow pathway leads from the doorway to the swivel chair within reach of a small table holding tubes of paints, paintbrushes, paint rags. The eye is drawn to the canvas secured to the easel. Geometrical markings cover the canvas, some coloured in a musty olive-green, greyish-blue, mauve-purple. The painting shows a superb refinement of skill, painted with control, with careful deliberation. If it is nearing completion, four or five phrases would be handwritten on a piece of paper sticky-taped to the easel.

> *Nearly; but Not. You're not what I thought you were. He Thinks He Knows. She thinks she Doesn't. If He doesn't get it, there's Nothing to Get.*

A visitor might see the house as that of an eccentric artist who had more important things to do than tidy up. She might be wondering, 'How can you live in this clutter? What's with all the dead flowers?' She might notice the packet of no-brand-name biscuits haphazardly placed alongside the designer glass vase. She might notice the frayed edges of the handkerchief clutched in the artist's hand, identifying a piece of torn-off Actil sheet. She would not know that somewhere in the house one could find fine embroidered handkerchiefs, linen tea towels, bath towels of Egyptian cotton, gifts from children and grandchildren never used.

The house is like a labyrinth, an art installation. The artist in her painting room is in the centre of the labyrinth, spinning her web around her.

The British artist Tracey Emin created an installation *My Bed*. Her unmade bed was removed, transported, rearranged and placed into an art gallery. Crowds lined up to stare at the tumbled sheets, used tissues, dirty underwear, cigarettes, empty vodka bottles, condoms, perhaps held in the fantasy of the drama that had created the tableaux before them.

After his death, Francis Bacon's shambled mess of a studio was dismantled, transported and reinstalled in the country of his birth. These private spaces made public may have promised to reveal the mind of the artist, as if somewhere amidst that disorder the mystery to the art could be found.

Very often, as I drove towards my mother's house, the thought would strike me: 'Who am I to visit Helen Brack, Helen Maudsley?' I am not a journalist, a gallery director, a curator. If I were not her daughter, I would not be paying her a visit. I am not a person of significance.

During the visit, Mum's conversation would be punctuated by uncensored asides. 'She asked the most daft questions.' 'So and so is just an idiot.' 'He's just a nobody.' 'She thinks she knows about John's work, but she doesn't.' 'He fancies himself as a real artist.' 'It's just decorative what she's doing. It's not serious work.' 'She's just pandering to what other people want.'

Sometimes I would offer my opinion. 'Well, her work is in a different genre from yours, Mum. It's a more accessible genre; besides, she is a performance artist. Your work demands a different way of looking.'

Driving home I would find myself consumed by a dull nothingness. I would see myself as worthless. It was not until a real conversation with another human being that my sense of myself would be restored. I could not explain it. It's not as if my mother had pointed her finger at me *telling* me I was worthless, and I knew it wasn't just that I was looking at myself through her eyes. It took me a long time to realise that the worthlessness I felt in the presence of my mother was what she felt about herself. In seeking a connection with her, I made myself susceptible to the worthlessness she unconsciously transmitted, and which temporarily relieved her of it.

She tells V:

I loved the house and garden, painting the rooms, selecting the furniture and the objects in the house. Early in John's career, when the children were little, I would spend days tidying up for an important visitor who had come to see John about his work. After all that tidying up, I remember one of the visitors saying, 'How nice to see a house so lived in.'

I was interested in cooking and loved making meals for people. I hated it when a meal was lovingly made and considered, but accepted by the recipient as trash. I never got over the time it took two days to prepare and cook a dinner with a duck. The two guests picked and poked at the dishes and after the dinner the lady of the couple said, 'I really don't like that sort of cooking. I prefer plain duck with apple sauce and mashed potatoes and peas. I'm only being honest.' John thought it was funny. I felt angry and defeated and never forgot it. The next day I got up, rallied myself and did everything again—the children, the painting and what needed to be done for the household. It could never be said that I was a warrior, which John certainly was.

V: Perhaps John could not have been a warrior without your help preparing him for battle, your consolation if the battle was lost, and your encouragement for the battle that would follow.

That was my job. I did it meticulously. I did all the business side of it, warning John not to give away a drawing, telling those gallery people that we would not be their stupid unpaid servants, you know. Even though we were both doing the same work painting pictures, my work was not given anything like the attention that John's work was given. I wondered if it was because I was a woman artist. In those days, gallery directors supported men artists who also had wives or girlfriends to jolly them along. When women's liberation came to Melbourne in the late 1960s, women artists formed a group. I went along, hopeful, but it turned out that these women artists were against the men artists just for being men. They didn't want to be taken seriously. They just wanted to be given the status of great artist, of high achiever—what many of the men artists wanted also, and which I had contempt for.

V: So you didn't join up with the women artists.

No, I didn't join up. I wasn't at all interested in shooting down the men artists I admired.

V: One of whom was your husband.

As both Helen Brack, wife of the artist, and Helen Maudsley, artist, more often than not Mum was invited to artist events as the wife of the artist, thereby receiving an entrée into a world from which other 'women artists' were excluded. If Dad did not want to go to one of these events, Mum went alone but the delight when someone showed an interest in her work could turn to indignation if it turned out that they were simply 'cosying' up to her, as she said, to find out something about Dad.

Several years after his death, she was speaking about her paintings when another panellist turned to her and asked, 'Is it true that you are John Brack's wife?'

'Never heard of him,' she said.

She says to V:

As I said, I didn't want to shoot down men artists whom I admired. And I certainly wasn't going to kowtow to John. I remember the first time he said he didn't want to go to an artist party. He was very taken aback when I said I would go without him. He expected me to stay at home keeping him company watching the television. I loved getting dressed up and going out. I loved talking to the other artist wives. I also had the credibility as an artist myself. Sometimes someone would ask me why John wasn't there as if I wasn't entitled to be there myself.

V: You felt that you belonged.

If John had come, he would have sulked all the way home.

In public Mum would claim her rightful place as an artist and an artist wife. In private Dad's needs took priority. When he was told to stop drinking, Mum worried that if we were drinking wine on

Christmas day, he would help himself to the bottle. It had been a lot of effort to get him off the grog, so I understood why Mum didn't want him tempted.

A few days before Christmas, Mum told me how she had bought several bottles of mineral water and different-coloured fruit juice, mixing them together in her kitchen laboratory. 'If I pour this into a wine glass, John will think it is wine. He won't know the difference.'

I assumed that Dad would be drinking Mum's concoction while we were drinking the real stuff, but it turned out that this was not to be the case. On Christmas day, we were offered what looked like white wine, red wine and rosé presented in wine glasses on a tray. If Dad was not permitted alcohol none of us would be permitted, including Mum herself.

She says to V:

Last night I woke up in the middle of the night, feeling guilty about my murderous thoughts about John. I remembered my fury with him for getting dementia, for not looking after himself, for needing all my attention. And then I lay awake feeling guilty about any number of things to do with the children.

V: You are tormenting yourself.

At least when I am painting, I am not feeling guilty.

Mum yearns to be free of the 'everyday guilt'. I doubt that she felt guilt about not protecting us from Dad's undermining. She endured it herself. No one protected her.

I remember one dinnertime. Dad, sitting up his end of the kitchen table, eating his steak, Mum sitting up her end, the four of us in the middle, finishing our chops. Dad was drunk. 'Look at your mother. Look at her. Isn't she despicable. Isn't she disgusting.' None of us could speak but Mum found her voice. 'Stop it John. Stop it. Not in front of the children.'

Dad would scoff at the everyday encounters that gave Mum pleasure. He did not have the temperament or the inclination to savour what delighted Mum and to share it with her. To her disappointment, he refused to accompany her on several trips overseas visiting the art galleries. She wrote wonderful letters, seven or eight pages of words crammed onto the page. *The café is run by a darling little German man with real old-world courtesy...The guards have the most glamorous dashing uniforms, pale-grey with an extraordinary comic version of a Russian fur hat.*

After Dad's death, I had imagined that for the first time in her life Mum could spend uninterrupted time on her own work and things she liked doing. I had not anticipated that a mythical aura is bequeathed to the recently deceased artist, an aura that entices the wife of the artist to make a space for herself in the halo of this mystique. Mum conscientiously responded to the invitations to promote Dad's work, giving talks, writing essays and opening exhibitions. She could relish the status of the venerated wife of the artist unencumbered by the presence of the artist himself.

She was free of her duties as a wife, but she was also free to be an authority on Dad's work. She spent hours not so much *looking* at his paintings but *deciphering* them, seeking to elicit his intentions as if the paintings were, like hers, seeking to be 'deciphered'. I do not know how she convinced herself that *The Block*, a painting of a butcher's block, was a reference to the Holocaust. When asked for justification from someone in the audience, 'Did you talk to John about his painting?' she retaliated with, 'Of course we did.' Later she would refer to the 'idiot' who asked the question. It was not just the appropriation of the Holocaust that alarmed us children, but the fact that she had attributed it to Dad. If we dared to query what we suggested were *her* interpretations of Dad's paintings, she would retaliate with something like, 'Now I know why people ask me why John hated his children so much.'

She says to V:

After John's death I was asked to give talks about his work and write articles for auction catalogues. I took this job very seriously, studying the paintings, taking notes, spending hours writing up what the painting was about. After giving a talk it was often disappointing. People would ask the most daft questions. They wanted to know whether John discussed his work with me, whether I had read what he had written, whether we had the same studio and watched each other painting. It was insulting. They didn't have a clue.

V: Perhaps they were wondering how you knew John's meaning of the painting.

They weren't. They were just being stickybeaks.

V: As you said, you knew what the painting was about from looking at it, not from what John said about it.

I knew what John meant. I mean, the nicest thing he ever did was in that last painting of the five Pinocchio figures. It was a way of thanking all of us for all the work we put into his career.

V: Just the fact of there being five figures?

It was obvious that the five figures represented the mother and the four children and that in putting us into the painting he was thanking us for what we had done for his work.

V: You needed John to make this acknowledgement. You wanted to be seen. You wanted to be acknowledged. And John made that acknowledgement.

No no, you idiot. I know what John meant.

One Sunday afternoon Mum gave a talk on Dad's painting *The Bar* at the National Gallery of Victoria. The painting depicts a woman at the bar with a mirror behind her. The mirror reflects the men drinking. A vase of poppies is on the bar. Well before the beginning of the talk the four of us daughters had seated ourselves in the audience along with several husbands and grandchildren. We were there to give her our moral support and to boost the numbers in the audience as Mum worried there would not be sufficient people turning up. She commenced reading the talk. Later she sent me a copy.

'Let's look at *The Bar* 1954. John was thirty-four and I was twenty-seven when he painted *The Bar*. In 1954 our fourth daughter was born, our first having been born in 1949, so John's suburban home life was dominated by babies and small children. Look at *The Bar* again. Can you see how all the hats at the top look like suburban roof tops? Stare again and can you see how those two light bits form a face?'

The face eluded me. I nervously wondered what others in the audience were thinking.

'Look at the barmaid; can you see how the man on the left matches her? A husband and wife. Can you see how the shape of the vase is womb-shaped? The bottles relate via the V shape to the barmaid; are they children?'

I wondered if Mum felt unnerved by the silence of the audience. She would have no way of reading whether they were following her.

'Then there are the flowers whose stems you hardly see but whose petals tremble, as it were. Is this not unlike the tremble of the embryo inside the womb? See the exaggerated size of the slurping man in the centre, and is this not like the baby learning to drink from a cup after weaning? The barmaid is the mother, the mopper-up of mess. See how the glasses become the children, cleaning, and is that forceful V image of the beer tap on the right side of the picture to do with engendering and potency?'

I dared not think what Dad would make of this.

'This picture is about the continuation of human life, but was never seen as such.'

She stopped reading and appealed for a response. 'This is interesting, is it not?'

I nodded. Others were nodding. She continued until the talk concluded, the audience clapped enthusiastically and then questions followed.

What *is* interesting is what is not said. The woman in *The Bar* displays her hands. Hands are very difficult to draw. Mum does not say that she made time from looking after the baby and three small children to pose as a model for the hands. She concluded her talk with, 'This picture is about the continuation of human life, but was never seen as such.'

To my knowledge, she had not seen it as such herself until Dad's comment many years after he painted *The Bar* when she returned from seeing a newborn grandchild.

'When I told John that I didn't understand why I was weeping over the new baby, he said, "You know what that is? That is the continuation of human life."' I wondered if she had remembered something Dad said about the Holocaust and attributed that to the painting called *The Block*.

After the talk, knowing Mum's need for reassurance, I told her how interesting it was and how well it was received, feeling the distaste of colluding in something I considered ludicrously improbable. Dad said himself that *The Bar* was a comment on Manet's painting *A Bar at the Folies-Bergère*. His focus was not on the mother of his children inside the house; it was on creating a place for himself in the History of Art.

She says to V:

John's painting *The Bar* is obviously not just a painting of a barmaid. It's a picture of me as the mother, the mopper-up of mess. It's John's acknowledgement of all the work that I was doing as a mother.

V: You looked at the painting, and you saw yourself reflected back. You needed John to see you and you saw that in the painting.

No no, that was what John had intended.

V: In not wishing to confront your disappointment that John did not thank you for what you did for his work, you told yourself a story that he had acknowledged you in the painting. In telling it to an audience and hearing their applause, you could convince yourself that John had given you the thanks that you craved.

No no, it wasn't like that.

V: If you release yourself from this self-deception, you will face the disappointment that John never told you what you meant to him.

No no. That is just rubbish.

And then, after a long pause, she says:

At least you're not saying what John would say.

V: What is that?

Can't you get that into your fat head. You nong.

*

In the time between the visits with V, I want to believe that she will consider what V is saying. I want to believe that she will weep for the loss that arose when Dad had dementia, for the loss after his death and for her disappointment that he never thanked her for all that she did for him.

In the next session she says:

I like to think that if John didn't get dementia he would have thanked me for all that I had done for him. He never thanked Dad for getting him the job at Melbourne Grammar.

V: You did an extraordinary amount of work for John's career.

Well, that's just what was expected of a wife. The wife looked after the husband as the breadwinner.

V: You are disappointed that John did not acknowledge all the work you put into his career but when I acknowledge you, you dismiss me as if you are resisting the very thing you seek. You belittle me for praising you, offering you comfort as if you are not worthy of it. You shut me off. You find it difficult to name your feelings. You either say 'I don't know' or deny them. You are your own worst enemy with your appetite for self-abnegation.

Well, who are you? I've never heard anyone speak to me like that.

In the next session she says:

I don't know. I wish I didn't feel this guilt, not just everyday guilt, guilt that I have done something wrong.

V: Perhaps you are feeling guilt that you have not lived up to the impossible demands you put on yourself. Perhaps you are feeling the unknown guilt that your parents passed on. The sins of the father passed onto the child.

Whatever it is, I just want relief from the feeling of the guilt.

V: What would it take to absolve yourself of the guilt?

I don't know. Now I feel guilty that I am taking up your time.

*

'It's an honour to have an exhibition at the NGV,' I said to Mum after the opening of her exhibition.

'Oh yes, it is an honour but it's tedious what you have to do beforehand. I just hope I've got everything right.'

Respectful articles were written about her work in major newspapers. She was interviewed on the radio, invited to give talks about her work. Despite the attention, she could not be coaxed into enjoying the success.

'There's been a lot of interest in your exhibition, Mum. It's fantastic, all the publicity.'

'I'll just be glad when the wretched thing is over.'

'It's marvellous, Mum,' I said, striving to generate some enthusiasm. 'So many people have been to the exhibition and Sasha wrote that lovely review. "A profound exhibition", he called it.'

'Oh yes, that *was* a nice review but what about the friends?'

'What about the friends?'

'Well, [name of friend] said, "The paintings are beautiful Helen, but I don't know what they mean." It's disgusting. And then a woman I went to school with invited me to lunch. She said she didn't understand the titles. She asked me to explain them. I mean, I ask you, the idiot. Some people are just daft. To think she had been some sort of professor at the university.'

'But lots of people have been terribly impressed. And you did all that amazing work without the support of Dad.'

In the silence after, I could see her considering her response.

'But you wouldn't say that to anybody, would you?'

To say that would damage the reputation of the important man.

How does she describe this to V?

Well, finally I did have an exhibition at the NGV with three other women artists. You just have to go along with what the curator wants. All this nonsense they go on with. It's so far removed from the actual job of painting. John hated that sort of thing, but you have to do it. I didn't see what all the fuss was about. It takes so much time away from painting. I was just glad when the wretched thing was over. People say the most daft things. Do you get your ideas from dreams? I mean, I ask you. One of the other women artists was traipsing around the exhibition with her mother and father, talking about the paintings. I wish my father had seen my paintings and understood them.

V: What would it mean if your father had seen your paintings and understood them?

It would mean that I wouldn't have self-doubt.

V: You invested him with that authority.

Whatever that means. I don't know.

Silence.

When John had self-doubt, it was my job to tell him not to be so ridiculous.

V: It wouldn't occur to you that John could relieve you of self-doubt.

I don't know. I never wavered in my belief in John as an artist. In his preoccupation with his work, he didn't have much time for mine. He was not an easy person to live with. No one really knew the difficulties of living with his depression and his drinking.

V: You could have left him.

Oh no. I couldn't do that. Not after that enormous effort in the early days getting John to be successful. I would not leave him for some young popsy to come in, swooping him up, getting all the rewards.

V: What were the rewards?

Oh, I don't know. His success. The fact that he was seen as a significant artist. The respect he was given, that little bit more money that came into the household. I am extremely glad that John has been successful. He was the right person with the right contribution at the right time.

V: And you were the right person to support him. His success was your reward for the work you put into his career.

It was very important for John to be successful. In those days most wives supported their husbands. It's just what you did. That's what my mother did. You just made do with the space you were given. John had a painting room in the house. My workspace was a board over a desktop in the sitting room. When John became head of the gallery school, he no longer needed work space at home, so for the first time in my life I had a painting room of my own. I didn't have to clear everything up at the end of the day. I could do bigger works. I could paint in oil paints not just watercolours.

V: Your painting had been limited by the space you had available.

That's just how it was. I knew from very early on that I would take a different approach to painting from John. While maintaining integrity of the task, John set his sights on meshing with the public, whereas people like me were deemed amateurs because we didn't aim to fit in with viewers. John needed to fit in with viewers. He needed to mesh with the public in order to sell paintings so we would have enough money to live on. I was just doing what I was meant to do in supporting his career.

V: As you said, you had not aimed to fit in with viewers. In ensuring that your work would require more from the viewer, you guaranteed that it would receive less attention than John's. If more attention had been given to your work, John would have seen you as taking the place that both you and he had designated to him.

No no no, it wasn't like that. John was a very significant artist. You're just like the others, too stupid to see what I am getting at, reading into it what you want to see. I supported John not because of any goodness but because it was in my interest to do so. It was terribly *much* in my interest that John was a success. He would have hated not being successful. I would have had to cope with his sulking and his misery, his complaints, his moaning about wanting to give up. He would have made our home life unbearable, not just for me but for the children.

V: You created elusive and enigmatic works that ask a lot from others to understand. Perhaps unconsciously, you ensured that your work was not readily understood because if more interest was given to it, John would see you as taking his rightful place, and in his woundedness he would have made your home life unbearable.

No no no. I wanted to paint what you call 'elusive and enigmatic' works.

V: Perhaps you could not have created these enigmatic works if you did not have the security of John's shadow in which to hide. While protesting against being in John's shadow, perhaps you are overlooking the necessity to hide in his shadow.

That's just rubbish.

*

At a concert Mum will loudly proclaim: 'The men cellists are just better than the women.' One of her granddaughters is a cellist.

In the second week of interviews for my daughter's first published book, Mum rang me to tell me that, 'Alice should stop all that nonsense publicity. She will be getting too big for her boots.'

If this was her response to her granddaughters, what would it have been for her daughters? We must have known not to venture into that space. She may not have said it explicitly but this is the message I received: 'If others want to be recognised, let them have it; they want it more than you do.' And yet, she herself had never forgotten that Ruth Muir got 93.75 for the music exam and she got 93.45.

*

She says to V:

People don't get the titles of my paintings and you don't seem to get what I am saying when I tell you that it was very important to John to be successful.

V: Perhaps you see the public space as belonging to the man. You grapple with your envy of women who dare to take up the space that you do not allow yourself to take. The woman who had an exhibition in Berlin for those decorative pieces she was making, not a serious artist like yourself. The women artists who wanted to be 'great artists', who had ambition which you had contempt for.

Well, so many women artists just do works that are decorative and pretty. Art isn't about beauty. It's about being serious. I just don't understand why serious people don't see the seriousness of my work.

V: Perhaps 'serious' for you requires untangling a complicated maze. In paring back the image and in writing longer titles, you were erecting a very sophisticated scaffolding around yourself. After spending so much effort devising such a scaffolding, it would be too confronting to face the fact that you could take it down. When you see others not putting themselves through such an elaborate process, it insults you. How can they get away with it? It affronts you that others are not covering themselves up as you are. Furthermore, they are getting away with it. You are protecting yourself against being known.

Long silence.

I recently did a series of four paintings called *There, but Protecting Against. Retiring into one's Head. And Ambiguity.*

V: Underneath the 'retiring into the head and ambiguity' there is a small child crying out to be seen and known and loved and understood.

A young man was asked to clean a chandelier. It took him hours to remove each piece of dangling glass, clean it and return it to its designated place. On being told to remove each piece of glass and put it back the right way around, he said, 'I'm out of here. I don't want no prism sentence.'

In erecting the elaborate scaffolding around herself, I see my mother as giving herself a prism sentence, resisting knowledge of the forces that had led her into the prism.

*

After Dad's death Mum received the gift of a novel which starts with a widow calling on her widowed neighbour, wondering if he, too, is lonely and if so, would he consent to sleeping with her—not for sex but for keeping their souls company at night. Mum could not be drawn on discussing the novel, but the title *Our Souls At Night* must have struck a chord for, since receiving the novel, 'Our Souls' appeared in the titles of her paintings.

Our Souls that meet; our Souls together.

Our Souls; not our Selves. And the Shoe. 2019

Our Souls, Together and in Communication.

Here and Now. For a Moment. 2019

At a birthday dinner in her eighties, Mum tells us that she has an announcement to make. 'I have a new friend.' She leads us to expect that the new friend is like the widowed neighbour seeking a way out of loneliness at night. 'Every day on my walk my new friend is waiting for me at the top of the hill. Sometimes he is not there.'

Her new friend is the moon. He appears in some of her paintings.

Looking down, Looking up at, Looking into. The Quarter Moon,

The Half Moon, and The Full Moon. The Leaf is the Lips. 2022

Mum finds what she is looking for. I want her to find what she is not looking for.

She did several paintings named *Shostakovich Waltz No. 2*. I want V to take her out of 'retiring into one's head and ambiguity'. I want him to gently take her by the hand, pull her up from the chair, place one hand on her shoulder, the other around her waist and twirl her around to the music of Shostakovich's Waltz No. 2. I want her to collapse in the chair, exuberant, exhilarated. Given that V would not swirl her around in a waltz, knowing she would lose her balance, I will have to find something else to release her.

She tells V:

On my trip overseas, I went to the art museum in Philadelphia every day for a week, getting to know the museum guards, chatting to them every day. On the last day of my visit, they invited me into the office where I was surprised to see that they had given me a farewell party with cups of tea and cakes. I didn't understand it. I thought they must have mistaken me for someone of significance.

V: Why else would they be giving you a party? They are telling you: you are a person of significance. They are showing appreciation for your friendly chats.

After a minor brush with another car, Mum told us the password for her bankcard 'in case anything happens to me'. I recognised the initials of the four of us daughters and the order of our birth. 'What is the Q in the middle?' I ask. 'Can't you see? The Q is for queen.' Despite her sense of herself as insignificant, I wondered if she also saw herself as Q for queen.

Mum's doctor had advised her to have a daily walk after a hip replacement. Since then, she had refused the advice to have a walking aid, subsequently falling several times at home and in the street. We had given her a walking stick, a walking stick with a fold-up seat attached, a walking frame. We considered sending her a postcard of Dad's painting, *A Walking Stick Makes a Good Companion*. 'The Queen has a walking frame,' I said, 'so did Dame Elisabeth Murdoch,' a woman Mum admired and was flattered to be mistaken for. Her response to a question from an aged-care assessor: 'No, I don't get mood swings' and then, her voice rising to a crescendo, 'I get thoroughly pissed off when one of the children suggests that I need a walking stick or a walking frame.' On our insistence she conceded to having an alarm button around her neck.

Mum interpreted *The Bar* as a commentary on her. She saw herself as the woman at the bar, 'the mopper-up of mess'. Dad's painting *The Chase* is of three girls running. We recognised ourselves. I have no illusion that Dad actually *saw* us and yet when Mum offered the painting to the NGV as a gift, we felt that she was giving away a piece of us, a painting that said we meant something to Dad. On hearing our objections, Mum reluctantly withdrew the offer.

Several years later, we heard that she had offered it to the Art Gallery of Ballarat. Again, we asked her to reconsider.

She tells V:

On Friday morning, all four of the children came to see me, not for a friendly visit but to persuade me not to give away John's painting *The Chase*. I don't know why they thought there was any point in coming to see me. I had already made up my mind. The darling man at the gallery had already accepted the painting, I could hardly go back and say he couldn't have it. On and on they went about how the painting meant something to them just because three of them were in it. They had never been so united. If I had kept the painting, they would have squabbled over whose turn to have it and for how long. As I said, the Ballarat gallery is the best place for it. It is a significant painting of John's. It deserves to be seen by more people than in a family home. Anyway, I was jolly glad when they left. As I told them, 'It's my painting, I can do what I like with it.'

V: You found the power to defeat them.

Six months after the gift of *The Chase*, the four of us received a group email from Mum's contact at the Ballarat gallery. He was writing to tell us that the Ballarat gallery was honoured to welcome our father's wonderful painting into the gallery collection. He was 'reaching out' to see whether any or all of us would be interested in speaking with *The Age* which would run the story 'as an exclusive'. He proposed that a photograph of the gallery director standing next to *The Chase* would be 'more interesting' with us included. We were warmly invited to lunch and a tour of the gallery.

The next day Mum asked me about the email from her Ballarat pal, professing not to know what it was about despite having given him our email addresses. I told her that we had clarified that the gift was from her and not from the Brack family, and that we had declined the invitation to take part in the publicity for *The Chase*.

Later that day I received an automatic text message from Mum's alarm button. A flurry of texts let me know that Mum had fallen in the street, that she had a head laceration, and that a bystander had rung an ambulance. A photo of the scene showed a forlorn, shrivelled figure slumped in the middle of the road, head bowed, blood trickling down her face. Blankets cover her legs, a bandage towel is wrapped around her head. A woman wearing protective gloves is dabbing at her face. Four or five people are standing around the seated figure. It was almost 5 pm on a Friday afternoon.

The ambulance arrived and Mum was taken to the hospital. Charlotte waited with her for several hours in emergency.

The next day I received a photo of the front page of *The Courier*. The entire front page was given over to a photograph of the Ballarat gallery director standing next to Dad's painting, the headline declaring: 'Ballarat Wins The Chase'. A short paragraph (story page six) states: 'The artist is renowned for his dour portraits of ordinary people that normally sell for millions but this key work has been donated by the artist's wife, Helen.' As readers were turning the pages of the newspaper, the artist's wife Helen was slumped in the middle of a suburban street, blood trickling from her head, having ignored the advice of her four daughters to have a walking stick, the same four daughters whose pleading she triumphantly ignored in donating *The Chase*.

I recalled the studio portrait of the two-year-old, dressed in a satin frock with Peter Pan collar, hair brushed, a bow tied in her hair, arms clasping a teddy bear. I recalled a photograph of the young woman taken by celebrated photographer Athol Shmith: hair permed, pearls around her neck, formally posed in a photograph required of a daughter of the Melbourne Establishment. I look again at the photo of the woman fallen in the street. A crumpled figure slumped, a bandage wrapped around her head instead of the crown befitting a woman who saw herself as Q for queen. There was something tragically King Lear-ish about it. Dad would see the little comedy. I can't see what that is.

She comes in to see V, a blue-black bruise down her face.

V: Oh, what happened?

It's nothing really. It looks much worse than it is. One minute I was walking across the road and the next minute I was sitting down with someone wrapping something around my head. People were standing around me. I don't know why they didn't help me up. I didn't ask them to be there.

V: You didn't ask them to be there, but you created a situation where they would put themselves there, putting yourself at the mercy of the public for help.

You're just as bad as John. I woke up in the middle of the night hearing him saying, 'Serves you right.' I am constantly thinking, how *could* I have done that, and why on *earth* didn't I do that? Why did I not hear what others were saying until after a disaster? Why could I see in hindsight but not in foresight?

V: So what is your explanation?

I just didn't think it would happen to me, not if I was especially careful.

V: You thought you would be immune to what other mortals suffer.

I don't know.

V: What is stopping you from asking for help? What is stopping you from seeing yourself as worthy of the kindness of strangers putting a bandage on your head, waiting until seeing you safely into the ambulance, the door closed and driven off to the hospital? What is stopping you from seeing yourself as worthy of a little celebration from the guards at a museum, showing their appreciation at having made a connection with them?

I don't know. My life is peppered with omissions and inappropriate moves and also my own ignorance and unawareness—expecting people would laugh at the funny parts of the speech I made and then ridiculed for missing the point. Expecting a friend would be pleased with a surprise visit and then when we arrived attacked by savage dogs, terrifying the children. Realising that the present I had given was somehow not right. More and more often I regret that I haven't been kinder to people, more thoughtful, more aware of other people's agonies, regretting my lack of patience, thinking they should just pull themselves together as I had.

V: We can torment ourselves with regrets, indulge ourselves with our misgivings, punish ourselves for what we did or didn't do. I am giving you some homework, appealing to your conscientiousness. I am asking you to be kind to yourself, to see yourself as significant, to recognise your achievement, to see your worthiness as a human being.

I don't know. I am not going to be kind to myself just by saying, 'I promise to be kind to myself'.

V: Very well, let me try another approach. You asked, 'How do we get permission for our innermost selves?' I am giving you permission to be kind to your innermost self. This is your homework, to at least think about what I am saying.

I don't know. It all seems too much right at this moment. Overwhelming.

In the next session she says:

You will be pleased to know that I have been doing my homework. Bill Nuttall exhibited my work at Niagara Galleries. I once told him that the only reason he shows my paintings is that this gives him access to selling John's work. 'Well, that's not actually true,' he said. 'They are very valuable works, very significant.' Now I actually believe him.

V: That is wonderful. You are giving Bill the respect he deserves. Perhaps your respect for Bill can extend to yourself, to me and to all human beings.

After a silence she hastily brushes back a tear, gathering herself together to say what she needs to say now.

I realise that I was very angry with Mum for depriving us of a grandmother who would have loved us. I have been wondering about the guilt she must have felt, the fear of being found out, the shame of being found out, the shame of the grandmother living in sin. I wonder whether her guilt was passed on to me. I now feel a blessing for being relieved of the guilt. I don't know how it happened.

V: Congratulations. That is marvellous.

In the next session she says:

I have been doing some research on Eddie Leonski.

V: Oh, remind me who he is.

He was found guilty of murdering several women in Melbourne in the 1940s. Dad was the psychiatrist who had been called upon to give him a psychiatric assessment. Leonski was sentenced to death. He was terrified of dying. It wasn't part of his job, but Dad made time to visit him in prison, and on the day of his execution he sat with him, holding his hand right until the end.

V: Perhaps you see me as holding your hand right until the end.

I don't want to think about the end.

V: You don't want to think about the end and yet I sense a reconciliation with yourself. As you said, you actually believed Bill when he said your paintings were significant. You are trusting that he means what he says. You are trusting your innermost self.

I do feel relieved to think that my paintings aren't going into the rubbish bin and all that effort has actually been worthwhile.

V: All that effort has been worthwhile.

A long silence.

V: That is wonderful. Congratulations. We have concluded our work together.

I feel a sort of sadness now, but thank you. Thank you, darling man.

V: Thank you.

V helps her with her coat and then holds her to him tightly in the loving warmth of an embrace.

Reflections

No one starts out in therapy knowing where it will take them. It's not just discovering what is underlying the conflict with one's boss.

No one starts out writing knowing where it will take them. I did not start out with this intention but now I realise that I have told my mother's story as the story of a woman who yearns to be seen and loved by her father, and my father's story as the story of a man reconciling with his mother.

How would I tell the story of how I came to be writing theirs?

My story starts with writing letters. My mother was too busy to hear about my day so I wrote letters to her. 'Darling Darling Mummy, tomorrow we have Rilidjus Inshrukshon.' Having never heard of a man called God, I thought I was telling her about this amazing man she didn't know existed.

My story continues with the closest I would ever get to my father, sitting for my portrait. As a child I sat very still thinking that if I moved, he would make a mistake. I saw him as all knowing, looking into me, seeing everything about me. Thirty years later I did not give him this omnipotence. As I sat watching him sketch, I kept my composure, aware of his failings, knowing he would never know very much about me. I wrote a letter telling him what it meant to me sitting for the portrait.

Before he drew portraits of my children, I reassured them that they did not have to sit perfectly still. Papa would not make a mistake. I took black-and-white photographs of the sittings, each child posed in front of the artist sketching. After developing the negatives, I discovered that the image was not what I had seen looking through the camera. It was a scrambled incoherence of faces, hands, pens, pencils, drawings, doorways. I had neglected to take the used film out of the camera. One set of photographs was superimposed over another.

Gazing at this muddled conglomeration I heard my father's voice, 'You dill.' As a way of counteracting his voice within me, I decided to print the photograph with an accompanying letter drawing attention to the mistakes with comments in red in the margin.

In pre-empting my father's criticism, I was telling him that I would not make him the judging omnipotent being. I pointed out the enigmatic mystery of the collage, a mystery that I could not have depicted had I set out to make it.

I do not know what my father made of the photograph with its written commentary below, but I do know that it meant something to him. The next time I saw it, it was hung on the wall framed behind glass. A painting had been relocated to make space for it.

By putting the letter into the frame my father had given me the gift of his acknowledgement. For my sixteenth birthday he had given me E.M. Forster's *Aspects of the Novel*, 'Yes, oh dear, yes, the novel tells a story', and H.W. Fowler's *Dictionary of Modern English Usage*. Until then he had never given me a gift.

I read my father's books. He said that, originally, he wanted to be a poet but had abandoned the idea as he didn't think he had the talent. I am not a poet but I have drawn on the work of poets and writers and what they say about writing. The writer William Maxwell says, 'My mother's sister told me that when my mother was twelve years old she used to go up into the attic and "write on her novel." So perhaps I am a projection of my mother's unlived literary life.'

Perhaps I am a projection of the unlived life of my father. What about the unlived life of my mother? 'But you wouldn't say that to anybody, would you?' my mother said in response to my remark that she did 'all that amazing work without the support of Dad'. For her, to 'say that' would be to cast aspersions on the reputation of the important man. For me not to 'say that' would be to deny one of the forces that had shaped me.

'How do we get permission for our innermost selves?' my mother asks in the title of a painting. In speaking of the private, I am giving myself permission to speak my innermost self. In speaking of the private, I am offering an insight into how my mother's deference to the important man had seeped into her work. In speaking of the private, I am living the unlived life of my mother.

When friends and acquaintances discover that I am the daughter of two artists I am often asked, 'Do you paint?' Besides talent, there are legacies we carry from our parents. There are 'the gaps left within us' by the secrets of others, the opportunity to repair something, to make amends, to make sense and give meaning to what is passed on to us like a baton.

'Now my journey through folklore is over...(I have) confirmation of what I already suspected—folktales are real.' It is not just quotes that I am drawn to but stories that resonate.

Something had fascinated me about the story of the Japanese man Yasuo Takamatsu who had learned scuba diving so he could go searching in the ocean for the body of his wife who had disappeared after the tsunami. For more than ten years he searched, putting himself in that space where his wife had disappeared.

In writing my mother and my father's dialogue with a therapist, I have put myself into the vastness of the ocean between truth and fiction and where they collide. I have put myself into that space between the death of my parents and my own death when my memories of them will disappear. Unlike Takamatsu, I was not looking for something that was lost but until I came to the end of the writing, or rather the ending came to me, I did not know what would emerge from within the depths of the writing.

My father said that he felt atavistic guilt for being so much more financially successful than his father. My mother was seeking atonement for her everyday guilt.

What about my own guilt? I felt guilt that my mother did not receive the recognition for her paintings that Dad had received, having worked so hard, doing all the housework, looking after Dad and looking after us children. She tells V that she felt guilt for getting pregnant, that it was her fault. Perhaps the guilt that I attribute to her is my guilt that I was the child she conceived and why she subsequently had to get married.

Writing transforms the writer. In writing the scene where V embraces my mother, I felt the warmth of his love and her need to receive it. In receiving his love I was relieved of the sense of betraying my mother in speaking of what she considered private. In writing and rewriting the scene where my father makes a cup of tea for his mother, I felt his nervousness in pouring the water into the teapot, putting the Tic Toc biscuits onto the plate, bringing in the tray. I felt his desire to offer something to his mother, to please her. As my father shed his grievances with his mother, I was shedding my grievances with him.

Now that I am nearing the end of this writing, I anticipate feeling bereft despite the achievement of having resolved something with my mother and my father. What can I do next? I wonder what would arise if I had a conversation with the writing part of myself. But even as I prepare to ask what to do next I know that the writing has to come from something deeper, something mysterious, something more elusive. We cannot look for it. It finds us. When asked what inspired her to write her novel, the writer said that the idea had come to her in the car on the way to her grandfather's funeral.

I know now that when we sit with the question we become receptive to answers that present themselves to us.

Perhaps I am looking for the girl I was. If could speak to her I would ask, 'Are you within me or have you gone forever?'

Postscript

In the beginning of this book I wondered what it would have been like if there was a boy in our family. I had invented a scenario where my father has a son with Sonya, a Russian dancer who has defected from the Ballets Russes.

As the book reached its final stage I emailed Sasha Grishin who had interviewed Dad in writing *The Art of John Brack*, which had been a valuable resource to me. I informed him of the forthcoming book. In an email response he observes:

Writing a monograph on an artist's work is a very different exercise to writing about a person's biography. I think that many people have different facades when it comes to other people. I am a different person to my wife and children than I am to my students and again different to my artist friends. I don't think that I am consciously aware of this, but many people have told me, for example, I appear to be a different person when I am speaking Russian from the person speaking in English.

Then he says this:

Your father, for me, was an incredibly kind person. I think about the number of times he would go down to Camberwell and buy for me a bottle of Noilly Prat extra dry vermouth when I was coming round, simply because I couldn't stand whiskey. He selected passages of poetry, esp Philip Larkin, that he wanted to discuss with me and would bring out paintings to talk about. This had nothing to do with our book and continued after the book was published. He showed me a great generosity of spirit and I was surprised when some other people spoke of negative experiences with him. His biggest compliment was when he said to me, if I had a son, I would have liked him to be a bit like you.

References

Abraham, N. (1987) 'Notes on the phantom: A complement to Freud's meta-psychology', *Critical Inquiry*, 13(2), pp. 287–292. Translated by N. Rand.

'Ballarat Wins The Chase', *The Ballarat Courier*, Friday 2 June 2023.

Burkhardt, B. (Editor) (2012) *Conversations with William Maxwell*. University Press of Mississippi.

Calvino, I. (2013) *Italian Folk Tales*. Penguin Books.

Camus, A. (1955) *The Myth of Sisyphus and Other Essays*. Translated by J. O'Brien. New York: Vintage.

Cane, S. (2013) 'On this day: First Australian Nobel Prize for Literature', *Australian Geographic*, 13 December. (Quote from Patrick White)

Flanagan, R. (2023) *Question 7*. Penguin Random House.

Fuller, P. (1993) *Henry Moore*. Methuen Publishing.

Grishin, S. (1990) *The Art of John Brack*. Melbourne: Oxford University Press.

Grishin, S. (2017) *Helen Maudsley: In praise of slow art*. Grishin's Art Blog 23, 18 November. http://www.sashagrishin.com/blog/archives/11-2017

Kafka, F. (1954) *Letter to His Father*. Translated by E. Kaiser and E. Wilkins. New York: Schocken Books.

Kafka, F. (1977) *Letters to Friends, Family, and Editors*. Translated by R. Manheim and E. Muir. New York: Schocken Books, p. 16.

Malcolm, J. (1994) *The Silent Woman: Sylvia Plath and Ted Hughes*. London: Penguin Books.

Maxwell, W. (1996) *So Long, See You Tomorrow*, Vintage International.

Merwin, W.S. (1983) *Opening The Hand*. New York: Atheneum.

Oliver, M. (1986) 'The Visitor', *Dream Work*. Boston, MA: Atlantic Monthly Press.

White, P. (1979) *The Twyborn Affair.* London: Jonathan Cape.

Winnicott, D.W. (1971) *Playing and Reality*. London: Tavistock Publications.

The image of *The Beach* is a photograph of a reproduction in:
Millar, R. (1971) *John Brack*. Melbourne: Lansdowne Press.

Acknowledgements

Special thanks to my writing group. To Sarah Tomasetti for initiating the group, to Annie Green, Fleur Glenn, Kate Derum, Mary Martin, Ann Drillich and Anna Taylor for responding so generously to my early work, for sharing their own writing, and for allowing me to see the possibility of publishing my work.

My deepest gratitude to Anna Rappoport for patiently holding space for me to recognise the significance of family secrets, to confront shame, and to give myself permission to find my own voice.

My sincere thanks to Nadine Davidoff for her superb editing: for seeing what the book was truly about, for respecting the integrity of the work, and for giving me the courage to trust the writing.

To Jenny Kemp, for conversations about being a daughter of artists, and for incisive feedback that changed the course of the manuscript.

To Brian Derum, for valuable feedback on early drafts and for his ongoing encouragement.

To Lindsay Brack, for conversations about his childhood with Dad, and for his short history of the Brack family.

To Sasha Grishin, for copies of tapes of his interview with Dad for *The Art of John Brack*, for references to Mum's work on his blog, *Grishin's Art Blog (GAB)* and for permission to publish his email to me.

To Sarah Sentilles, writing mentor, for inspiring workshops and for encouraging imaginative possibilities in writing.

To Terri-ann White at Upswell Publishing, for her enthusiastic response to the pitch of the manuscript and for seeing its potential.

To my sisters, Vicky, Freda and Charlotte, for sharing their experiences of childhood, for offering their perspectives on our parents and for being the only others in the world who truly *know* them.

Finally, to my husband, Ross Williams, and to my daughters, Rose and Alice, for their love and for their ongoing support of the quiet work of writing.

About Upswell

Upswell Publishing was established in 2021 by Terri-ann White as a not-for-profit press. A perceived gap in the market for distinctive literary works in fiction, poetry and narrative non-fiction was the motivation. In her years as a bookseller, writer and then publisher, Terri-ann has maintained a watch on literary books and the way they insinuate themselves into a cultural space and are then located within our literary and cultural inheritance. She is interested in making books to last: books with the potential to still be noticed, and noted, after decades and thus be ripe to influence new literary histories.

About this typeface

Book designer Becky Chilcott chose Foundry Origin not only as a strong, carefully considered, and dependable typeface, but also to honour her late friend and mentor, type designer Freda Sack, who oversaw the project. Designed by Freda's long-standing colleague, Stuart de Rozario, much like Upswell Publishing, Foundry Origin was created out of the desire to say something new.

www.ingramcontent.com/pod-product-compliance
Lightning Source LLC
La Vergne TN
LVHW041928090826
845145LV00017B/2231

* 9 7 8 1 7 6 4 2 3 9 7 3 8 *